PRAISE FOR BIZARRE LAWS

'A fascinating list of absurdities ... an extraordinary work ... remarkable and praiseworthy ... an extraordinary achievement.'

Sir Michael Parkinson CBE
Broadcaster, journalist & author

'Well assembled and written ... an enjoyable and fascinating book.'

William Roache, OBE
Actor, 'Ken Barlow' in Coronation Street

'This is a terrific book, entertaining, informative and quirky.'

HH Nigel Lithman KC - former Crown Court Judge

'An endlessly fascinating journey ... Impeccably researched ... impossible to put down. A truly remarkable book.'

Tracy Borman
Chief Curator for HM Historic Royal Palaces

'Monty Lord's brilliant writing makes this book accessible to everyone.'

The Rt Hon Sir Robert Buckland KBE KC MP
Lord High Chancellor of Great Britain (2019-21)
Secretary of State for Justice (2019-21)
Solicitor General for England and Wales (2014-19)

'An engaging and light-hearted portrayal of the judicial system over the centuries, presented by an extraordinary 17-year-old.'

Cherie Blair CBE, KC

'A rich spectrum of tasty clues to our nation's story ... A jolly read.'

Major General Alastair Bruce of Crionaich OBE VR
The Governor of Edinburgh Castle

'A curious, comical and highly entertaining read, full of eccentric laws and customs that have led to our rich legal heritage.'

Lubna Shuja
President of The Law Society of England and Wales

BIZARRE LAWS OF THE UK
FOR KIDS
MONTY LORD

LONDON & MANCHESTER
YOUNG LEGAL EAGLES

Copyright © 2023 by MONTGOMERY LORD

All rights reserved. No part of this book may be reproduced, stored in a retrieval system, or transmitted in any form or by any means — electronic, mechanical, photocopy, recording, scanning, or other — without permission in writing from the publisher, except by reviewers, who may quote brief passages in a review.

The right of Monty Lord to be identified as the Author of this work has been asserted by him in accordance with the Copyright, Designs and Patents Act, 1988.

A CIP catalogue record for this book is available from the British Library.

ISBN 978-1-916605-08-4 (paperback)

ISBN 978-1-916605-09-1 (hardback)

ISBN 978-1-916605-10-7 (audiobook)

ISBN 978-1-916605-11-4 (eBook)

ISBN 978-1-916605-12-1 (large print)

Cover Design: Rachel Jackson

Illustrations by: Priya Ajith

Published in England, United Kingdom, by Young Legal Eagles®
a trademark of Young Legal Eagles Ltd.

www.YoungLegalEagles.com

To Bradley,

Keep up the GREAT work & NEVER give up!

I dedicate this book to every school student, ever. Just when you think life closes a door on you, around the corner another one will always open.

I also dedicate this book to hard-working teachers everywhere who make it their life goal to inspire children and make their dreams come true. Those they teach will go out into the world and achieve great things. Thank-you especially to my former headteacher Tony McCabe from St. Joseph's RC High School. You are all the real heroes!

To Frankie, thank-you for sticking around and always supporting me.

With my very best wishes, Monty Lord. (2025). :)

"Rights are like muscles. If you don't exercise them, you lose them!"

Monty Lord

CONTENTS

Foreword	IX
Preface	XI
Intro	XIII
1. An Englishman's Home Isn't His Castle	1
2. Animals & Fish	15
3. Apparel, Accessories & Appearance	37
4. Assault, Injury & Death	57
5. Behaviour	65
6. Courts	81
7. Death & Execution	91
8. Food & Drink	117
9. Foreigners	125
10. Fun & Games	135
11. Indecency	149
12. Justice	155
13. Money	173
14. Parliament	179

15.	Police	189
16.	Punishment & Torture	199
17.	Religion & Puritanical Behaviour	221
18.	Roads, Pathways & Waterways	235
19.	The Royal Household	247
20.	Trades	263
21.	Witchcraft & Other Sorcery	269
Acknowledgments		277
About Author		281

FOREWORD

As I write, I see on the national news young people in schools up and down the UK daring to protest about the 'school rules' that they perceive to be unfair. Some young people are protesting that certain schools are insisting that skirts are worn to a specific length with the belief that this undermines a person's liberties, others are suggesting that young people should be able to leave lessons when they like to go to the toilet. Headteachers across the country are being interviewed stating that uniform policies are about ensuring that everyone looks the same (uniform) regardless of background or wealth and that school have a role in trying to teach young people discipline in terms of controlling their bladder!

As a Headteacher (in fact, Monty Lord's former Headteacher nonetheless!) I watch on and wonder what the Monty Lord of 2123 would make of this in 100 years' time. Will this time in history sit in the 'Indecency' chapter of later edits of this book?

As you read you will be taken back in time to the strange traditions of the past and some that that still live on today. I hope that this will develop in you the same type of enquiring mind that we saw develop in Monty and drove him to spend endless hours in the British Library Reading room to research and investigate these strange traditions and myths.

I hope you enjoy this 'tongue in cheek' book as much as I did and share it with your friends and family...because if you don't, you might end up getting the 'Red hot poker treatment' (actually, I think this might be illegal now – check out page 109!).

Tony McCabe
Headteacher
St. Joseph's RC High School, Horwich, Bolton

PREFACE

It was a warm spring afternoon, and I found myself sitting on the train, travelling down to see the Prime Minister at No. 10 Downing Street, London. A gentleman dressed in a sharp suit sat opposite me, occasionally popping his head out from behind the newspaper he was reading in front of his face. An article on the front page of his newspaper attracted my attention. It was about a rarely used ancient law. I pulled out my phone and began to do some research into the matter. It was this moment that sparked my further research. This continued on the journey home, exhausting my phone battery. Half a year later, I finally finished my research for this book. I say that as I look at several folders of unused material on my shelf, just ready for a follow-up book.

I have always had an interest in the law. I started writing this book at the age of 16. Now 17 and with a burning passion for children's rights. I have given several speeches about children's rights at Amnesty International HQ in London and the United Nations in Geneva.

Have you ever heard a bizarre saying and wondered about its origins or even whether it is true? Things like whether it is illegal to kill a ghost or that playing football or cricket was once against the law? Within these pages, you will find the answers to those questions and some other curious customs we have developed over the centuries. This book seeks to inspire, amuse, shock and educate. Yes, all at the same time.

During my endless hours spent researching for this book in the British Library reading rooms and other locations around the UK, I had to absorb so much information. What started as a small research project expanded to fill a large portion of my computer hard drive. At times, researching our ancient laws felt like Alice in Wonderland falling down the rabbit hole. Probably the most challenging aspect of my research was each time I came across an ancient manuscript written in Norman French or Latin. I can tell you now that Google Translate isn't much help!

Ultimately, I found it a very exciting process, especially when I came across the occasional golden nugget ... those laws that are so bizarre, even their very existence is questionable.

Whether you love history, the law or even just learning about bizarre facts, I would advise you to visit your local library and museums. They aren't boring or stuffy places (well, some are!) and you can learn a lot, not just from the books but also the staff working there.

I wish you well. Enjoy reading, and please drop me a note to let me know how you found the book.

Monty Lord
Lancashire, England (2022)
www.MontyLord.com

INTRO

Our legal system is a mish-mash of customs, traditions and laws passed over the centuries to protect the people and regulate society.

A quick browse through the archives and ancient manuscripts produces some astonishing finds of laws passed to control activity and behaviour at the time, which now seem completely absurd. In many cases, these laws are still active. Some are outlandishly bizarre, almost like they were created to amuse and entertain those, like us, who may read them centuries later.

The law books can become filled with these old laws. Over the years, these have become so outdated that they eventually lose relevance and start to appear absurd. These ancient laws can't litter the law books forever, so, over time, new laws are passed, and old ones are removed (repealed).

This book contains 21 chapters, separated into the various aspects of our British life, each containing some fantastic examples of bizarre laws. Many more outlandish laws, claims, local myths and legends came to light whilst researching this book. There are too many to mention and they are perhaps material for a future book.

A fellow author told me to explain to my readers how to use this book. Well, frankly, that's entirely up to you. However, I will point out this book is multi-functional: a compendium of wisdom, truth and absurdity; a reference book; a door stop; an insect swatter; a shield to protect your eyes from stray Norman arrows; or an implement to softly repel inquisitive hobgoblins ... the decision is entirely yours!

What you're going to find between the covers of this book will hopefully also give you an insight into a lot of the history of the United Kingdom. Laws are, after all, passed to deal with issues that concerned people at the time they were made. The insight it provides us is invaluable.

"Ultimately, law is just common sense with knobs on."
(The Rt Hon Lord Sumption, OBE, FRHistS, FSA)

One last thing ...

Before you delve into the pages of this book, there is one more thing I would like to mention. As this book deals with the topic of law, it has been written in a way which seeks to avoid the constant use of the terms '*he*' and '*she*'. Irrespective of what pronoun you use, the gender you were born, or how you presently identify, no offence is intended when I refer to one specific gender. The law has historically been written using male pronouns. Please bear that in mind. Also, please realise that the nature of this book takes a tongue-in-cheek look at the absurdity of some of our ancient laws. In today's society, many of these may appear wrong and particularly harsh towards certain groups of people.

I would hope that most readers would take a commonsense approach and realise that it's illegal to hang, draw and quarter people, shoot Welsh people in Chester, or even convey a corpse in the back of a taxi. It goes without saying that none of the information contained within this book constitutes legal advice and is provided for general information purposes only.

Chapter One

An Englishman's Home Isn't His Castle

In this chapter, we peel back a further layer of the laws prohibiting our activity in the home. This particular area of law has littered the law books over the centuries. It's amusing to see that many of the laws in this area passed during the Victorian age were more concerned with the upkeep of your home and ensuring nothing you do affects the quality of life of your neighbours.

Only Permitted to Keep One Lunatic in Your House

A law passed in 1774 ensured that property owners were only permitted to keep one 'lunatic' per residence. If you wanted to keep more than one lunatic in your house, you were required to apply for a licence to keep them. It's certainly a bizarre law. The law was passed to regulate what we now refer to as psychiatric hospitals.

Previously, such hospitals were referred to as lunatic asylums. The sad fact is that whilst they started to grow in popularity during the early 1600s, as private institutions, there were no laws regulating how they were run. There was, in common law, a power to *"confine a person disordered in mind, who seems disposed to do mischief to himself, or another person."*

There were many stories of horrific abuse and patient mistreatment. One matter of particular concern was that of wrongful confinement. Quite often, rather than divorce a wife, it was easier and less dishonourable for the husband to have her committed as a 'lunatic'.

This law imposed a penalty of £500 for any person *"concealing or confining"* more than one insane person without a licence. So, you were permitted to keep a 'lunatic' just so long as you didn't plan on keeping a collection of them.

This law was repealed just before Queen Victoria came to the throne.

AN ENGLISHMAN'S HOME ISN'T HIS CASTLE

You Can't Fire a Cannon Within 300 Yards of Your House

"Glorious day, Mr. Binnacle! Glorious! No-one sleeps this morning. Put in a double charge of powder" bellowed Admiral Boom in Mary Poppins as he ordered his rooftop cannon to be fired. Unfortunately for Admiral Boom, he would be committing an offence under the Metropolitan Police Act (1839).

This law states, *"No person, other than persons acting in obedience to lawful authority, shall discharge any cannon or other fire-arm ... within three hundred yards of any dwelling house ... to the annoyance of any inhabitant thereof."*

For Admiral Boom or anyone wishing to fire their cannon again, the penalty is a £200 fine. If you were thinking of heading to a popular auction website and purchasing a cannon and some cannon balls, please be advised that this law is still live on our statute books.

Illegal to Keep a Pigsty at the Front of Your Property

I'm afraid the lyrics are going to have to be changed as follows:

"Old McDonald had a farm, Ee i ee i o. And on his farm he had some pigs ... but they were hidden from public view to avoid prosecution."

The problem is that Old McDonald was permitted to keep his cows and some chicks, but if he wanted to keep his pigs, a law passed in 1847 provided some strict guidelines to follow.

It permitted a person to keep pigs, so long as the pigsty was out of public view. I can't imagine too many people have been prosecuted over recent years for keeping pigs on their front lawn, to the annoyance of other residents.

Amusingly, this law was only repealed as recently as 2015.

No Shaking Your Rugs in the Street

For those houseproud homeowners living in London, there's bad news for you. There's every likelihood you've been unknowingly breaking the law for years.

A law from 1839 banned the shaking of carpets, rugs or mats in the street.

AN ENGLISHMAN'S HOME ISN'T HIS CASTLE

The penalty for shaking your rugs in any London street was initially a fine of forty shillings for each offence. The fine has now risen to £200. Bizarrely, the law does permit you to shake or beat your doormat in the road, but only if it's done before 8am. This section of the law was introduced to prohibit 'nuisances' on the streets of London.

As an amusing side note, the law also says that it's an offence to *"throw or lay any ... fish, offal, or rubbish ... into any well, stream, or watercourse, pond, or reservoir for water."* This would prohibit anglers from returning any caught fish back into the water.

Don't Order Your Servant to Stand on Your Window Sill

This next bizarre law from 1847 makes it illegal to order or permit any servant or cleaner to stand on the window sill to clean or paint it ... unless it's a basement window.

It states, *"Every occupier of any house or other building or other person who orders or permits any person in his service to stand on the sill of any window, in order to clean, paint, or perform any other operation upon the outside of such window, or upon any house or other building within the said limits, unless such window be in the sunk or basement."*

This law was only repealed as recently as 2015.

Illegal to Have Unsecured Window Boxes or Flower Pots

This somewhat outdated law may be of interest to those not living in bungalows.

A law from 1847 stated, *"Every person who fixes or places any flower-pot or box, or other heavy article, in any upper window, without sufficiently guarding the same against being blown down"* is guilty of an offence.

This means that you must ensure that any window boxes or flower pots are firmly secured so as not to risk falling onto the heads of passers-by in the street below. This law was repealed very recently, in 2015.

Illegal to Hang Your Bed or Safe Out of an Upstairs Window

It is an offence to place any heavy article in any upper window without securing it.

This isn't just for flower pots and window boxes. It also means that you can't hang your bed out of an upstairs window ... although quite why you would want to is probably more bizarre than the law prohibiting it. Also, if you were considering hanging a large cast iron safe out of your upstairs window, re-enacting a scene from an old Tom & Jerry cartoon, that's a definite no-no.

It is Not an Offence for Someone to Park Their Car on Your Driveway and Leave it There for a Week

It is not an offence to park a car on a stranger's driveway and leave it there for a week or even longer. By that same token, a stranger can park their car on your driveway. Legally, there is very little you can do about this.

The Manchester Evening News featured an interesting article on 16th March 2022 about a concerned householder living near Manchester Airport. He had arrived home to discover a Range Rover parked on his driveway. He had given no prior permission for it to be there. The parked car blocked access to his garden, and he could not get his bins out, ready for collection. He reported the matter to the Greater Manchester Police, who informed him there was nothing they could do because it was not a criminal offence.

Parking on private land is classed as a civil trespass and a nuisance. It is not a criminal offence because it is not parked on the public highway. This is similar to a case reported in June 2018 in which a woman living in Hull arrived home to find someone else's car parked on her driveway. In that instance, Humberside Police could be of no help.

It is for this same reason that you may look through the back windows of your house & see a stranger sunbathing on your lawn. It's a civil trespass.

Apples and Blossom

In May 2022, the media reported on the case of a proud garden owner who was becoming increasingly angry after having to vacuum their garden each day due to the annoyance of the neighbour's blossom tree covering it with blankets of blossom. Believe it or not, tree disputes with neighbours are pretty commonplace.

If you're the victim of a similar circumstance and covered daily with your neighbour's blossoms and leaves, there's not much you can do other than clean it up. That's Mother Nature for you.

But what if your neighbour's tree overhangs your garden and regularly drops fruit and branches, is the fruit yours and are you able to take it? You may be surprised to learn that you may be guilty of theft if you do.

You are permitted to trim the branches or foliage that overhangs your garden at the point where they cross your boundary. But you may not take any fruit from those branches or flowers that sprout from them.

Perhaps rather annoyingly, your neighbours are under no legal obligation to prevent the blossom, leaves or fruit from falling from their trees into your garden. They are not required to clean them up either.

However, if you keep hold of any fruit that falls from their branches, even if it falls onto your garden, in law, this could

AN ENGLISHMAN'S HOME ISN'T HIS CASTLE

be considered theft. Bizarrely, this even includes if you collect the fruit and broken branches whilst cleaning your garden and putting them in your bin. This is because it's your neighbour's property, and you are treating it and disposing of it as though it's your own property.

Interestingly, it is not a criminal offence to plant in your neighbour's garden or any other garden for that matter.

In 1945, the Bournemouth Evening Echo newspaper reported on the case of Mrs. Irene Graham of Boscombe. She recalled a German prisoner of war who worked on her garden weekly until he returned to Germany at the end of the Second World War. She'd described him as a *"nice friendly chap."* Although, she was rather displeased when crocuses came up in the middle of her lawn the following February, spelling the words '*Heil Hitler*'.

Flying Drones Over People's Homes

It's a lovely quiet summer's day. You're sat outside sunbathing and enjoying the British air in the privacy of your garden. Suddenly you hear the distant hum of what sounds like an approaching swarm of bees. With some trepidation, you turn your gaze to the sky and notice a black box hovering above your garden. It's a drone!

Drones can be flown anywhere in the UK that is not restricted airspace, provided some rules and laws are followed.

Whilst the law permits drones to be flown in unrestricted airspace, there are a few prohibitions to restrict drone movements.

The problem is that the majority of drones you see flying around these days are smaller drones weighing less than 250g. The restrictions are more flexible on these smaller, lighter drones. For example, you can fly them closer to people and even fly them over people lawfully.

So, back to the scenario where you're sitting relaxing in your garden, reading a good book and hearing the distant hum of an approaching drone. You look at the sky and see that it's a small drone weighing less than 250g. The drone hovers for a good 10 minutes over your house, apparently watching you. I'm sure we can all agree that this would be very uncomfortable. Most likely, you would stop what you are doing, make some angry gestures towards the drone, and take cover indoors until the drone has gone away. Is there anything you can do?

Unless you live within 5 km of an airport and provided the drone isn't being operated dangerously, then even though it appears to be ruining the privacy of your garden, there isn't much you can do about it.

Houses In Scotland Can Not Have a Pink Front Door

For some other unlucky householders, their choice of paint colour may get them into a spot of bother. In October 2022, one Edinburgh resident was left pink-faced when she received a letter from the City of Edinburgh Council, insisting that she repaint her front door white or face a fine of up to £20,000.

Miranda Dickson living in the historic Georgian area of the city, received this shocking request from the local council

AN ENGLISHMAN'S HOME ISN'T HIS CASTLE

shortly after repainting her front door the colour pink. The council informed Ms. Dickson that her door was not in keeping with the local historical character and ordered her to paint her front door to a more "*suitable*" colour which should be "*dark and muted.*"

Confused with this request, she sought clarification from the council on what colour she should choose to paint her front door. The council stated that they were "*unable to advise.*" The council's request seems to have come about after receiving just one complaint from an anonymous resident living near Ms. Dickson.

After Ms. Dickson initially refused to repaint her door, the council issued an enforcement notice against her for failing to apply for planning permission for her door colour.

Illegal to Put Rubbish Into Someone Else's Bin

Imagine walking along the street and eating a sandwich. You finish your sandwich or drink and decide (hopefully) to do the community-minded thing and not throw it down as litter. You notice that the local council have put no bins in the street where you are. Not to worry, it's bin day, and all the residents have placed their bins out in the street. Do you throw your rubbish discretely into one of their wheelie bins and quickly walk off?

Before you do that, consider the following. The illegal discarding or depositing of waste materials and rubbish products on land or water is an offence. You could be guilty of littering if you dispose of your rubbish in someone else's bin without their permission. The law sees this as antisocial behaviour, as it's classed as fly-tipping.

It is an offence to throw down, drop or otherwise deposit and leave litter in any place open to the air, including private land. The same law also applies to placing your rubbish in bins belonging to offices and shops and, of course, one of those large yellow builder's skips that we seem to find on many streets these days.

Illegal to Remove Items From Someone Else's Bin

There's an old saying ... "*One Man's Trash is Another Man's Treasure.*" But can it be your treasure? If it's someone else's

AN ENGLISHMAN'S HOME ISN'T HIS CASTLE

rubbish and they've thrown it in the bin, are you legally allowed to take it?

Technically it is theft if you take something from another person's bin without their permission.

According to the Theft Act (1968), property continues to belong to a person unless it has been abandoned entirely. When people place their rubbish into a bin, they haven't abandoned it. They have left it there, intending for the council to come and remove it. When the council has removed it, it is no longer the property of the person who put it in the bin. They cease 'owning' it. It then becomes the council's property to dispose of in the usual manner.

The law also accepts that if a person intends to throw something away and wishes to claim no further ownership of it, this would be considered abandonment. If something is 'abandoned', it has no owner legally, so if anyone else takes it, they would not be guilty of theft.

Illegal to Put Your Wheelie Bin Out on The Wrong Day

It's midday, and as I look out of my window, I see several neighbours have already dragged their wheelie bins out to the pavement. It's not bin collection until tomorrow lunchtime. People live such busy lives that it's often ideal to move the wheelie bin to the front of the house, ready for collection when you remember and get a chance to do it. Is that wrong? Apparently, yes, it is. As hard as this is to believe, some councils in the UK have classed a bin wheeled out to the pavement when it's not collection day, as fly-tipping.

Councils can issue a fixed penalty to householders who fail to comply with their local waste collection rules.

There have been cases in the past where councils fined householders £110 each for putting their bins out too early or wheeling them back too late.

Chapter Two

ANIMALS & FISH

There are some incredulous loopholes in our great legal system. The laws surrounding animals and fish provide some great examples, from the mundane to the entirely insane.

Of course, it's not just the animals themselves that the law protects, but also the forests, woodlands and their natural habitats. However, these laws were introduced to protect these areas, not so much for the good of the animals but to protect the hunting rights of the noblemen.

This chapter addresses some of the absurdities in the law surrounding animals and fish. Surprisingly, the laws were more straightforward in the Middle Ages, but the punishments were much harsher. These days, whilst the penalties are less severe, it is far easier to fall foul of the law unknowingly.

Leave those swans alone!

Illegal to Own a Sturgeon But Not a Pet Tiger

According to an ancient law, all whales and sturgeon found within the kingdom, whether alive or dead, are property of His Majesty The King. This includes any beached whales. Over time, this law became interpreted to mean that any whales or sturgeon found must first be offered to the monarch, who would then decide what should happen to them. Historically, anyone who discovered a wreck or royal fish would have to declare them to the 'Receiver of Wreck'.

In 1322, King Edward II passed a law called *Prerogativa Regis* (Of the King's Prerogatives). Under this law, all whales and sturgeon may be considered 'Royal fish' and property of the monarch of England. This would now also include porpoises and dolphins. This law is still live on the statute books, although the monarch's automatic entitlement to all 'Wreck of the Sea' was removed in 1894.

In June 2004, Robert Davies from Llanelli in Wales had caught a sturgeon fish in Swansea Bay. He was aware of this ancient law and promptly contacted the Queen's Receiver of Wrecks, offering the sturgeon to Her Majesty. The Royal Household sent a message to Mr. Davies indicating that The Queen had declined the fish and suggested that Mr. Davies was entitled to *"dispose of it as he saw fit."*

Davies then drove to Plymouth to sell the sturgeon at auction. In the meantime, government officials had alerted the local constabulary, Devon and Cornwall Police. The police attended and stopped the sale of Davies's 10-foot-long 120kg sturgeon fish on the suspicion that it was being sold illegally and that Mr. Davies was in breach of the ancient law *Prerogativa Regis*. Davies had, in fact, arranged to sell the sturgeon to a local restaurant for £700. It was accepted that everyone involved had acted in good faith, especially as the Royal Household had indicated that it would be okay for Mr. Davies to sell the fish as his own. Being the focus of all this attention, the sturgeon finally ended up in the Natural History Museum in London.

Illegal to Touch a Pelican

It is an offence to touch a pelican within the Royal Parks and surrounding open spaces. You may be interested to know that it would also be illegal for you to ride a pelican. A law was passed in 1997. making it an offence to *'feed or touch any deer or pelican'*. It is also an offence to interfere with any plants or flowers within the Royal Parks. This conjures up imagery of Alice in Wonderland in the Queen's rose garden.

Illegal to Not Carry a Poo Bag Whilst Walking a Dog in Daventry

Imagine a small and inquisitive child, strolling alongside his parents, who drops his bag of toffee-nut chocolates on the pavement. He quickly gathers them, puts them back in the bag, and continues walking. Now imagine his parents' horror of finding out later that the contents of his 'sweetie bag' are no longer what they once were.

Laws covering dog poo are relatively recent. Thankfully, we are a long way from the days of Tudor England when people would pour their raw sewage out of the top windows of their houses onto the streets below, often covering unlucky passers-by. Under a 1996 law, failing to clean up after your dog became an offence. You could receive a fine of up to £80, but if the matter proceeded to court, the fine could increase to £1,000. This law was repealed in 2005, and local authorities now regulate enforcement against dog fouling.

In December 2015, Daventry District Council in Northamptonshire introduced a law, which requires all dog walkers to carry a spare poo bag to dispose of their dog's excrement. It is an offence to fail to comply. You could be fined £100 or up to £1,000 if the matter proceeds to court. Council workers can stop dog walkers and check whether they carry a spare bag. It also makes it an offence not to remove dog poo immediately. This applies to all public open land in Daventry, whether or not warning signs are displayed.

Interestingly, no legislation currently requires horse riders to clean up any horse poo from the road or pathways. However, they are encouraged to do so. Horse poo doesn't pose the same health hazard as dog poo. This is because horses, as herbivores, have a plant-based diet, and their excrement doesn't contain the same dangerous bacteria as that of a carnivore/omnivore dog.

Illegal to Walk More Than 4 Dogs in Daventry

A new bylaw passed by West Northamptonshire Council came into effect on 1st November 2022. It makes it illegal to walk more than four dogs at the same time in Daventry.

The council introduced this law to promote 'responsible dog ownership' in south Northamptonshire and Daventry. There appears to be no specific reason as to why the number was capped at four and not five or even ten dogs.

For those found breaking this new law, they face a £100 fine for each occasion.

The Killing of Swans is Illegal

Not just whales, sturgeon, dolphins and porpoises belong to the monarch; His Majesty may also claim a right over all wild, mute swans found in open water. The Crown has held the royal prerogative over these swans since the 12th century.

This isn't all swans, just the mute swans (*Cygnus olor*). The UK is home to 3 different types of swans; mute, whooper and Berwick swans. The most common swan in the UK is the mute swan. In reality, the Crown only exercises royal prerogative over swans on the River Thames and its tributaries and he is not the only owner either. The King shares his right with the Vintners' Company and the Dyers' Company, both City of London livery companies.

Since the 12th century, swans have been seen as a status of wealth and nobility. They were the mediaeval equivalent of owning an expensive car. Swan meat was seen as a delicacy at royal feasts and would be served whole and still feathered, often with a lump of smoking incense in its beak. Records show that forty swans were delivered for King Henry III's royal banquet at Winchester during Christmas 1247.

In today's world, those who choose to capture or kill a mute swan, must be sick and deranged. Quite rightly, such a person ought to be punished. This is provided by a law passed in 1981, as mute swans are now a native species and continue to be protected by law. This law makes it an offence to keep or kill them, which is punishable with a £5,000 fine.

Handling Salmon in Suspicious Circumstances

Imagine being arrested for walking down the high street carrying a large salmon under one arm. The good news is unless you're causing some sort of public nuisance, you're unlikely to be arrested for this. Although the wording of a law passed in 1986 would undoubtedly make it appear that was the case. Part of the law says '*Handling Salmon in Suspicious Circumstances*'. This law was expanded in 2009 to include many different types of fish, including trout, eels, lampreys, smelt, freshwater fish and not just salmon. It makes it an offence for any person in England and Wales to receive or dispose of salmon when they believe or should have reasonably suspected that the salmon had been illegally fished. The maximum sentence for this offence is two years imprisonment.

The law wasn't passed to punish those who physically handle salmon in a suspicious manner whilst walking along the street. It was introduced to reduce salmon poaching.

Deer, Oh Dear ... That's The Death Penalty

Following on from the Norman Conquest, King William the Conqueror decided to designate great swathes of the English countryside as his Royal Forests. These were his personal hunting grounds. The Royal Forests were so vast that they enveloped not only the woods but also villages and wastelands.

During the reign of King Henry II, around 30 per cent of the country was set aside for royal sport. In 1184, he passed a law called the Assize of the Forest, and this was followed by another law a few years later in 1198 by King Richard I. These set out the forest laws but with some very harsh punishments including blinding and castration for anyone caught poaching deer or boar in the King's Forest. He declared that no person could carry bows and arrows in his royal forests, and dogs were required to have their front claws removed to prevent them from hunting game. Court records from 1209 show that an individual named Hugh 'the Scot' was accused of poaching in the royal forests. He escaped and hid in a church, fleeing a month later, disguised as a woman.

The ill-feeling towards the King for using the forests for personal gain is shown in the Magna Carta signed in 1215. It banned all previous harsh punishments like mutilation, hanging, blinding and castration. It also severely restricted the Crown's ownership of the forests.

In 1217 the Charter of the Forest was drawn up by King Henry III, along with his modified version of the Magna Carta. This sorted out many of the previous grievances caused by the earlier Forest laws and reduced punishment to a heavy fine or a year and a day in prison.

In 1722, King George III passed a law called The Black Act. It got its name from the poachers who blackened their faces to disguise themselves. This one law created so many offences carrying the death penalty. It made any form of hunting in the royal forests punishable with a fine. Those who committed further poaching crimes were transported overseas to the colonies. Bizarrely, if you were found in the royal forests with a blackened face, your punishment was death.

No such gruesome punishments await those found guilty of poaching under the modern-day Deer Act (1991).

ANIMALS & FISH   23

Death Sentence If Found In a Forest, With a Blackened Face

Hunting was a pastime enjoyed by both Kings and commoners for centuries. In the early days, hunting was a necessity, part of our daily fight to survive within the animal kingdom.

Poachers would often hunt at night. To disguise themselves, they would blacken their faces to provide additional cover from detection. In response to this sharp increase in poaching, a law was passed in 1722 called The Black Act, so named in reference to the poachers' practice of 'blackening' their faces. This law made it an offence for anyone to hunt, kill, wound or steal deer in a forest, chase, down or Royal Park. The penalty for a first offence was a fine. For a second offence, the offender would be transported overseas to the colonies.

It also made it an offence to just be found in a forest with a blackened face. It was assumed you were there for poaching. The penalty for such an offence was death.

This law caused as much astonishment at the time as it does now that we look back upon it. It was known as the 'Bloody Code' because it introduced the death penalty for over 350 criminal offences. You would be hanged for things like damaging an orchard or a garden. Anyone caught conspiring to commit any of these offences or rescuing anyone imprisoned for these crimes would also receive the same death sentence.

King George IV repealed the Black Act on 21st June 1827.

Keeping Bears and Lions for Baiting

Bear-baiting, cock fights, dog fighting and fighting chimps were all the craze back in 16th century England. Spectators could watch dogs, chimps, bulls and bears all fighting to the death. These horrific animal gladiatorial games typified 16th and 17th-century entertainment.

In 1656, Oliver Cromwell ordered London's main bear-baiting arena to close, deeming it a lazy and immoral pastime. It soon re-opened and even had onsite ale houses. Bear-baiting was eventually banned in 1835. However, this failed to stop both dog and cock fighting.

During Queen Victoria's reign, the authorities decided to crack down heavily on such activities. In 1839, the Metropolitan Police Act was passed. Section 47 of the Act states, "... *every Person who within the Metropolitan Police District shall keep or use, or act in the Management of any House, Room, Pit, or other Place for the Purpose of fighting or baiting Lions, Bears, Badgers, Cocks, Dogs, or other Animals, shall be liable to a Penalty.*"

The penalty was a fine of up to £5 and possibly imprisonment for up to one month, with or without hard labour. This law was repealed in 2007 when it was replaced by a new law which makes no specific provision for bears and lions.

An Offence to Take a Rabid Dog on a Bus or a Corpse in a Taxi

Rabies was finally eradicated from all UK animals except bats in 1922. The last case of an imported un-quarantined animal with rabies was in 1970. The last recorded rabies case in the UK was in 2012. The individual had contracted the virus after being bitten by a dog in South Asia. It wasn't always this way. Britain experienced a sharp increase in dog owners during the 19th century, and by 1895 there were 672 cases of rabies in humans recorded in England.

The law bans anyone with a notifiable disease from travelling on any form of public transport, including taxis and buses, without first notifying the driver that they have a disease. Some examples of 'notifiable diseases' range from the severe and exotic, like the plague, rabies and leprosy, to the other end of the scale, to things like food poisoning. This is covered by a Control of Disease law passed in 1984. So, the next time you catch a taxi and feel you have a bit of a dodgy tummy, don't forget to inform the driver first.

It is up to the driver whether they agree to transport you.

When it comes to buses, that's a different matter altogether. If a bus driver knows you wish to travel with a notifiable disease, they can not allow you to board the bus.

This same law would also extend to any animals under your care. So, if you wanted to travel on-board a bus with a rabid dog on a lead, the driver would not be able to allow you on-board. In the worst-case scenario, and you happen to die before getting to your destination, you must also consider that your corpse may not be transported by taxi. A Public Health law from 1936 prevented carrying corpses and people suffering from infectious diseases in taxis, on vessels and aircraft, and other on-shore vehicles.

This does raise the curious question of what would happen if a passenger suddenly died during their taxi ride? Does the driver pull to the side of the road, open the door and drag the recently deceased person out of their taxi and onto the pavement?

In Kent, Cockerels are Not Permitted to Crow Within 182.88 Metres From Any Human Habitation

If you've ever lived on or near a farm, you may have been rudely awoken at first light each morning by the crows from the resident cockerels. If more than one cockerel is kept in an enclosure, they tend to compete with one another, raising the volume even further.

It is these crows that quite often give rise to neighbourly complaints in rural areas.

The local authority in the agricultural village of Biddenden, in the borough of Ashford, Kent, passed a law banning anyone from keeping cockerels closer than 200 yards (182.88 metres) to any human habitation.

Illegal to Incite Your Dog to Bark in Morecambe & Heysham

It's fair to say that we are a nation of animal lovers, especially dogs.

One law found in the 1907 Rule Book for Morecambe & Heysham makes it an offence for owners to incite or encourage their dogs to bark in public. This can even be caused through something as simple as throwing a bone for Fido to fetch. Fortunately, this law only covers the area near the seashore in Morecambe & Heysham.

I suspect this law was introduced to reduce noise pollution in the local area. According to the Lancaster City Council, this particular law was revoked on 8th December 2006.

Perfectly Legal to Sell & Purchase a Deadly King Cobra as a Pet

Through a bizarre loophole in the law, ordinary people can go to a pet shop in the UK and purchase any number of dangerous animals, amphibians, reptiles and all sorts of things that quite frankly would give you nightmares just thinking about them.

It is perfectly legal for a pet shop to sell and for us to purchase any rattlesnakes, King Cobras or deadly pit vipers. This is a common occurrence on our high street each day. They are being sold openly at pet shops, risking public safety. The current law governing the ownership of such animals came into force in 1976. This law allows pet shops to sell such dangerous creatures to be kept as pets. It also permits the purchase of them. The law does require the new owners to register the deadly pets with their local councils. The council will then inspect the premises and ensure that there is no risk of harm and that the animals can be kept safely by their new owners. However, they can only do this if the new owners get in touch with them. In many cases, this is just not happening. Many owners either don't bother to contact their council and get a licence to keep the dangerous animal, or they aren't even aware they need a licence.

Bizarrely, there would be no issues in purchasing a King Cobra. Their venom has multiple dangerous effects on the body. Its bite affects the central nervous system, causing debilitating pain, blurred vision and eventually paralysis and cardiovascular collapse. A coma and death follow shortly after due to respiratory failure.

In theory, you can purchase the most dangerous animals, including a crocodile. However, you do need to declare it to your local authority and have a licence. More than 100,000 wild animals such as crocodiles, alligators, Komodo dragons and monkeys are sold yearly in UK pet shops. So, the next time you feel something under the duvet at night and wonder whether it's just your imagination, it could be something more sinister altogether. Perhaps your neighbour's deadly Viper has decided to explore further afield.

I shall end this topic with an amusing anecdote showing just how dangerous even the smallest of animals can be. The Manchester Evening News reported on a bizarre workplace incident in 1875. A group of women were working in a south London factory when a mouse frantically ran across a work table. The women screamed, and complete confusion followed. Hearing their screams, a gallant young man came to their aid and grabbed the mouse. Unfortunately, the mouse escaped his clutches, scurried up his sleeve and out through the neck opening of his shirt. Surprised by this turn of events, the young man opened his mouth to utter some words. The mouse darted straight into the man's mouth. The shock forced him to swallow the mouse. Undoubtedly the mouse eventually died but not before killing his unwitting host. As the Manchester Evening News reported in graphic detail, "... *the mouse began to tear and bite inside the man's throat and chest, and the result was that the unfortunate fellow died after a little time in horrible agony.*"

Monkey Business

This next story, whilst not a law ... and I also hope it's not a custom, is an episode in our history that is too good to leave out of this book. We turn our attention to the townsfolk of Hartlepool in the North East of England, otherwise referred to as the '*monkey hangers*'. Today, we can happily drive through the Channel Tunnel or hop on a plane to visit the Eiffel Tower or sit along the banks of the River Seine eating a French baguette. The French! We have enjoyed a mutual love-hate relationship for centuries. If it's not food, football teams or fashion, there are a great many other differences between our two proud nations. But despite our centuries of death, crusades, conquering and mistrust, we stand side-by-side to protect each other.

It hasn't always been that way. During the Napoleonic Wars (1792-1815), mass public hysteria targeted hatred towards our old enemy, the French. Anything from France was treated with deep suspicion. In 1805, during the height of these Wars, a peculiar incident occurred one stormy day in an old fishing village on the North East coast of England. A French ship crashed into the shore, causing its sole survivor to jump ashore. He was quickly captured by the locals, who recognised the ship's markings as of French origin and immediately suspected him of being an unkempt, hairy French spy. For many of the locals who had never before seen a Frenchman, they naturally assumed landing ashore in a French ship, he must be French. The Frenchman was chattering gibberish, which the locals assumed was French. They promptly held a trial and found the Frenchman guilty of spying, hanging him on the beach.

ANIMALS & FISH 31

There was one problem in this trial. The Frenchman wasn't a Frenchman. In fact, he wasn't a man at all. As the sole survivor of the shipwreck, he was the ship's mascot, a monkey. Unfortunately for this monkey, none of the locals had seen either a Frenchman or a monkey before. They assumed the hairy monkey was a French sailor trying to spy on the British. We don't know whether this story is fact or fiction. It has gone down as a local legend, and to this day, the monkey remains the official mascot of Hartlepool's football team. The mascot's name is H'Angus the Monkey.

The Angry Parrots

Parrots have brought us centuries of entertainment, love and fun. Although sometimes they can get a little mischievous. It is this side of their personality and the resulting consequences that we shall look at now. In an amusing but equally absurd case from 1898 in London, we see a large fight break out in public caused by nothing more than a small parrot. The facts were reported on at the time in the newspaper, the Falkirk Herald.

Two friends, Arthur Crowe and George Tibbett, were seated at a table having a drink in a Blackfriars pub with a German lady. Another regular to the pub was Mr. Brambani, an Italian ice cream seller. He strolled into the bar to relax and have a drink. The pub's landlord kept a parrot behind the bar, and Brambani had been trying to teach the parrot to speak Italian for some time. On this occasion, the parrot apparently made a foul-mouthed reply. Whatever this parrot replied was enough to provoke Crowe and Tibbett into a fight. They believed the words had come from Mr. Brambani. They thought Brambani was making a rude remark about the German lady sitting at their table. Despite Mr. Brambani's protestations that the real culprit was the parrot behind the bar, Crowe and Tibbett challenged him to a fight and demanded an apology. It is reported that the parrot excitedly carried on swearing.

Brambani, sensing imminent danger, quickly made his escape and ran into his nearby sweet shop. The affronted two men and German woman pursued him and were quickly joined by a small mob. Mr. Brambani's nephew tried to explain what had happened and appealed for calm. Instead, he was pelted with bottles of ginger beer and glasses from the sweet shop counter.

Police Constables Greenway and Hunt arrived on the scene and arrested Crowe and Tibbett. The German lady had already made her escape. They were both jailed for a month. We have no further information on what happened to the parrot. Still, I suspect it remained in the pub due to the entertainment it brought.

Parrots have been kept by many pubs and ale houses over the centuries as a friendly and exotic form of entertainment for their customers.

Cats and Dogs Arrested For Spying

During wartime, the public paranoia rises to such a heightened degree that we can even believe our neighbour is an enemy spy. But what about the next-door neighbour's cat or their dog? Over the years, there have been some curious examples of such episodes of paranoia. In one of our more bizarre moments of history, during the First World War, British intelligence officers even suspected two cats and a dog of spying for the Germans in the allied trenches.

What raised this suspicion? According to records, the 36th Brigade of the 12th Division observed the cats and dog. They were repeatedly seen crossing the British trenches, so the matter was formally recorded in an intelligence log. This official record states, "*Two (2) cats and a dog are under suspicion, as they have been in the habit of crossing our trenches at night; steps are being taken to trap them if possible.*" As bizarre as this would seem, it's important to look at the matter in the context of the paranoia during wartime operations.

Their paranoia was well-founded. Records also show us that in 1908, the German army considered attaching camera devices to carrier pigeons to take aerial photographs. This is only five years after the first flight by the Wright brothers. As it happened, homing pigeons were used extensively throughout wartime to pass messages between the trenches and the command structure. An example of a famous homing pigeon is that of Cher Ami (French for 'Dear Friend'). It was donated by the British to the US Army stationed in France, who used Cher Ami to send messages to allied forces. The pigeon was later awarded the Croix de Guerre for bravery by the French after it sent messages from a trapped allied battalion in 1918, despite itself being injured.

Pigeons were also used during the Second World War by the Belgian spy Jozef Raskin who worked with the MI14 (Secret Pigeon Service) of the British Military Intelligence. He sketched maps of enemy lines and placed these inside small tubes on the legs of homing pigeons, which flew the intelligence information back to England.

Cats, dogs and pigeons weren't the only non-human spies we recruited. During World War One, the Admiralty's Board of Invention and Research looked for a way to detect the increasing number of German U-boats. They sought the help of a circus showman with his performing sea lions. They set about training sea lions to swim behind German U-boats to give away their locations to allied naval command. All seemed to go according to plan in the initial trials in a Westminster swimming pool. However, once the sea lions were sent out into the open sea to test their tracking skills against Royal Navy submarines, it became apparent the plan was doomed to fail. They became too distracted by schools of fish and would disappear for hours at a time.

Animals on Trial

The paranoia of guilty cats, dogs and other animals wasn't just confined to 20th-century warfare. It has been evident throughout our history.

We now look at the bizarre case of the 1861 trial of a game cock. This came about after a coroner's inquest was held in Leeds on the 4th of October 1860 on the body of 19-month-old Mary Tuckett. Sadly, Mary had died from injuries resulting from what was described as a 'ferocious game cock' belonging to the young boy Joe Parkinson.

The bird had for some time become an annoyance in the neighbourhood by flying at residents' heads. The coroner determined that the game cock had flown at Mary's head and knocked her over. As a result, Mary sustained multiple injuries from her fall and bled profusely for several days afterwards.

The headwounds became infected, which led to an abscess, resulting in inflammation of her brain, from which she later died. The trial was reported in The Observer newspaper and indicated that the jury's recommendation was for the bird to be killed at once. Mrs. Parkinson, the mother of Joe Parkinson, promised that the bird would be killed in front of some jury members.

Even earlier than that, there was a case in Chichester, England, in 1771 of a dog being placed on trial. The dog in question was called Porter and was charged with killing a hare. He was found guilty. He was sentenced to be hanged from a beam in the corner of the Chichester courthouse.

Welsh Atonement

An ancient Welsh law states that if you killed a cat or dog belonging to another person, you must fulfil an act of atonement. To show your remorse by atoning for your wrongdoing, you must hang the dead animal by its tail so that the tip of its nose touches the ground. To complete your atonement, you must also pour wheat over the animal's body until it is fully covered and no longer visible.

Chapter Three

Apparel, Accessories & Appearance

In this chapter, you will find fantastic stories about facial hair and laws passed to stop us from wearing indecent, immoral and extravagant clothing. They even had to pass laws to regulate our footwear. For some reason, our ancestors enjoyed walking around in clown shoes as long as planks of wood.

The next time you go outside, at least you won't be faced with the nonsensical decision as to whether you should wear a top hat or a woollen hat. The law may just decide for you!

Illegal to Wear an Indecent Tunic or Long, Pointed Footwear

Some of our earliest laws dating back to 1337, were passed to preserve decency and restrict items of clothing to particular classes of wealth and social rank. With the increasing imports of clothing and culture from overseas, there was a growing feeling that fashion was becoming more outrageous.

From the middle of the 14th century, this change in clothing styles could be noted in footwear, which had become more pointed and unnecessarily long over the previous decades. Whereas footwear had often been buckled, there was an increase in the more ornate design and use of embroidery and lacing.

It is believed that The Pope once tried to ban these pointed shoes. These became known as crackows, poulaines or pikes. The shoes became so elongated that towards the end of that century, the French poet Eustache Deschamps remarked that wearers had taken to walking sideways like crabs.

In 1363, King Edward III passed a clothing law. It detailed the style of clothing that each different social class was permitted to wear. Laws continued to be passed to regulate the length of shoes. The nobility was allowed 24" (61cm) pointed shoes; gentlemen could wear shoes measuring 12" (31 cm) long, and merchants were permitted 6.5" (17 cm) in length.

One hundred years later, King Edward IV passed an extensive clothing law in April 1463. It's also the first law that prohibits the use of the Royal colour purple. Men began wearing their shirts so short that codpieces were required to ensure a gentleman's groin would not be visible. It insisted that a gentleman's privates and bottom were covered by his coat. Offenders were fined 20 shillings (£650 in today's money) for unnecessarily exposing themselves.

It wasn't just the clothing. This law also addressed the shoes which had become so ludicrously long over the last century. It ordered that *"no knight under the estate of a lord, esquire or gentleman, nor any other person, shall wear any shoes or boots having spikes or points which exceed the length of two inches."*

The punishment for wearing what we now consider clown shoes was a fine of 3 shillings and 4 pence (just over £100 in today's money).

This 1463 law was repealed in 1604, so feel free to wear those 2-foot-long shoes next time you go shopping.

Illegal Not to Wear a Bobble Hat on Sundays if You Are Poor

Towards the end of the 16th century, knitted woollen headwear started going out of fashion. Around the same time, England saw a sharp decline in the wool trade whilst the public turned to the new favourites of cotton and silk. This posed a severe threat to the English wool industry.

In 1571, Parliament sought to put a stop to this by passing a new clothing law known as the Cappers Act. This law was introduced to provide a much-needed boost to the English wool industry. It required most males over six, to wear a woollen cap on Sundays and holidays.

As bizarre as this law might seem to us at first glance, it was even more peculiar because those who refused to wear the woollen hat received a fine of 3 shillings and 4 pence for each day it wasn't worn. This sadly meant that many poor people, who couldn't even afford to buy the hat, were liable to be imprisoned for non-payment of the fine.

Fortunately, after 26 years, Parliament decided to repeal this law in 1597, and we no longer needed to wear woollen caps.

Illegal For a Gentleman to Appear on the Public Highway Wearing Upon his Head a Tall Structure Having a Shining Lustre and Calculated to Frighten Timid People

Various people have thrown their hats into the ring over the years to be accredited as the inventor of the top hat in the UK. Whilst we can not say exactly who the inventor was, we do know from records about one of the first appearances of the top hat on our streets. Legend has it that the inventor of the top hat was John Hetherington, a haberdasher of the Strand, London, who produced what he referred to as a 'silk hat'. This was based on the stiff hat worn by horse riders.

Mr. Hetherington decided to wear his hat for the first time on the streets of London. And so, on 15th January 1797, he stepped out of his shop in the Strand, introducing his new fashion item to the public. Wow! No-one could have anticipated the public's response to his new item of headwear. The furore this caused led to Mr. Hetherington being arrested and taken to court on a charge of conduct likely to cause a breach of the King's peace, in particular, *"appearing on the public highway wearing upon his head a tall structure having a shining lustre and calculated to frighten timid people."*

In court, the officers of the Crown gave evidence that several women fainted at the sight of the headwear, whilst people booed, children screamed, and dogs yelped. The youngest son of a local shoemaker was pushed over by the ensuing crowd causing him to break his right arm. In his defence, Hetherington stated that he had not violated any current laws and was merely exercising his right to wear a headdress of his own design. He was bound over to keep the peace and forced to pay £500 (equivalent to £43,562 in 2021).

Half a century later, Queen Victoria's husband, Prince Albert, revived the popularity of the top hat.

Illegal to Hire a Maid Wearing an Old Silk Petticoat

By the start of the 17th century, maids and women-servants had started to dress in clothing that was considered above their social standing. This was causing such a headache to the aldermen of the City of London that they decided to pass a law to restrict these fashion excesses. On the 21st January 1611, the City of London Court of Common Council passed a law about the clothing that maids were permitted to wear. Official records show the rationale behind the passing of this law.

It was against the law for any householder within the City of London to hire a maid or woman-servant if she wore *"any gown, kirtle, waistcoat or petticoat, old or new, of any kind of silk stuff... nor any other stuff exceeding the price of 2 shillings and 6 pence per yard; nor any kersey exceeding the price of 5 shillings a yard; nor broadcloth exceeding the price of 10 shillings a yard."* It also restricted the wearing of *"any silk lace or guard upon her gown, kirtle, waistcoat or petticoat, or any other garment, save only a cape of velvet."*

Quite how the householder would check the value of silk per yard of their maid's petticoat is beyond me.

Beware of 'Persons With Great Beards' and Those Wearing 'Outrageous Breeches'

The City of London decided to pass its own laws for those who lived and worked within the City. In the Court of Common

Council, the aldermen passed a law against '*persons with great beards*'.

The same law told inhabitants of the City of London wards to be suspicious and keep a vigilant eye for anyone seen wearing '*outrageous breeches*' and to report offenders.

Illegal For a Woman to Encourage a Man to Marry Her by Wearing False Hair, High Heels or Make-up

It is said that Queen Elizabeth I passed the following edict, "*Any woman who through the use of false hair, Spanish hair pads, make-up, false hips, steel busks, panniers, high-heeled shoes or other devices, leads a subject of her majesty into marriage, shall be punished with the penalties of witchcraft.*"

This edict has been repeated so many times throughout historical text. Yet, I have been unable to find any evidence of this edict ever having been made officially by the Royal court. All laws and the majority of edicts, particularly from the time of Queen Elizabeth I, would have been thoroughly documented. We are unable to say, therefore, whether this edict is true. Nevertheless, it did reflect many of society's views from the time. Indeed, around that period in our history, many laws were passed to control how people dressed and their general appearance.

Another fictitious law that has become a legend is that of the supposed 1770 Hoops and Heels Act, also referred to as the Matrimonial Act. This Act was supposed to provide legal authority for husbands to divorce their wives if they had been seduced into marriage by the use of perfume, make-up, high heels and other forms of 'deception'.

In this case, we can say with absolute certainty that there never was any such law.

Laws Restricted What Maids Could Wear to Work

This bizarre 1611 City of London law banned many more things than just silk. It restricted what a maid could wear on her head.

Maids were prohibited from wearing any lawn, cambric, tiffiny, cobweb-lawn, white silk-cipres or linen cloth worth more than 5 shillings per elne (45 inches). Farthingales (underskirt expanded by a series of circular hoops) were also not allowed to be worn, and women were not allowed to wear whalebone or wire stiffeners in their bodices and sleeves.

The City aldermen didn't stop there. They also set strict rules about what a maid could wear in her apron. They were not allowed to be made out of silk, lawn, cambric fabric, or any other material that cost over 2 shillings and 6 pence per yard. Aprons were not permitted to be excessively wide or have any edging, lace or fringing. The wording of this law listed items from head to toe that were prohibited. The next on the list of banned items was stockings. Stockings made from worsted, jersey or silk were banned. Spanish-leather shoes or shoes with Polonia heels were forbidden. Shoes were also not permitted to have any stitching, rose or ribbon for the shoe strings.

For a first offence, a maid or woman-servant would be fined 3 shillings and 4 pence. For a second offence, the fine was 6 shillings and 8 pence. Half the penalty would be paid into the parish poor fund, and the other half would be paid to the informer. This scheme to reward informers would undoubtedly have led to much money paid to the parish poor fund. If the maid failed or refused to pay, they would be prosecuted for debt and imprisoned until they could pay.

Fancy Dress

Each year, across the length and breadth of the British Isles, thousands of people who are not members of the armed forces choose to dress in various military uniforms. They are, of course, attending Halloween parties, fancy dress parties, military re-enactments, and not to mention numerous student parties.

It became illegal to impersonate a soldier, sailor, Royal Marine or airman, even at fancy dress parties, under a law passed in 1906. There was quite a stiff penalty for those caught doing so. It could have ended in imprisonment. This law was repealed in 2008. So, partygoers may once again breathe a sigh of relief. However, not for long, because they may have realised there are still laws on the statute books preventing the unauthorised wearing of military uniforms.

A law passed in 1894 during the reign of Queen Victoria still makes it a crime for any civilian to wear the uniform of the armed forces without proper authorisation, in a way that brings contempt upon the uniform after falsely wearing it. It permits wearing uniforms for those acting in theatrical productions, such as HMS Pinafore.

Under the Army Act (1955), it used to be an offence to wear authentic or replica military decorations to deceive another. However, this law was repealed in 2006. This has left the door wide open to those Walter Mitty characters we hear so much about in the media. I'm referring to those committing the immoral act of wearing fake military medals in public, known as 'Stolen Valour'.

You are now wiser about attending parties dressed in military uniform. But how about attending instead dressed as a police officer? At the expense of ruining your party, I now have to tell you that it is also an offence to dress in public as a police officer. The Police Act (1996) creates the specific offence of impersonating a police officer.

The police will not take too kindly to you wearing a police helmet you may have purchased online. For such an offence, you could end up going to prison. Although, you may wish first to check that the arresting officer is not a random stranger also dressed in a fancy dress costume.

Interestingly, I see no mention in the law about whether this must be a current military or police uniform, but common sense surely dictates that you can't be arrested for dressing as a Norman soldier.

Women Not Permitted to Remove Their Hats at Thetford Town Council Meetings

In May 2016, the market town of Thetford in Norfolk was thrust into the national spotlight with media coverage over an 800-year-old dress code and a row over double standards. For centuries, women attending official Thetford Town Council functions must keep their hats on throughout the occasion. After loosening the rules in recent times, women were allowed to remove their hats but were first required to seek the permission of the mayor to remove them. Gentlemen needed no such permission to remove theirs.

In 2016, a female councillor complained about this, raising concerns about double standards and gender inequality. Councillors attending ceremonial meetings and whilst at civic events must wear traditional attire. This consists of long blue robes and black cocked hats. Even this didn't appease one female councillor who branded the rule change as "*outdated*" and "*demeaning*." The mayor at the time defended the rule and stated that they were "*just maintaining traditions.*"

By January 2017, it was reported that the tradition (gender inequality issue) of removing hats at formal Council events had ended. The rule had changed, and councillors, male or female, were all now required to keep their hats on during ceremonial meetings. Should anyone now wish to remove their hats, they are first required to seek permission from the mayor.

You Must Pay a Lump Sum For Any Facial Hair

Like makeup and clothing, at various times throughout our history, it seems that we have fallen out with facial hair. This is probably similar to how things go out of fashion these days, from hairstyles to designer jackets and even our names.

In 1447, King Henry VI passed a decree to ban moustaches and required men attending the Royal court to shave their upper lip every two weeks.

It is said that a beard tax was imposed on the people by King Henry VIII, forcing every man to pay a tax if they had a beard. There was a sliding scale of how much a person had to pay depending upon their wealth and social status. The larger a person's beard, the more money they were required to pay for it. Wearing facial hair during Tudor times symbolised a person's wealth and position in society. This all sounds very bizarre, doesn't it? Of course it does ... because it's simply not true.

It doesn't seem so far-fetched in the context of all the other bizarre laws passed centuries ago. However, like the supposed law banning make-up by Queen Elizabeth I, there is no evidence of this 'law' ever having existed.

We know that during the reign of King George I, there was a beard tax, just not in our country. I'm referring to the beard tax imposed in 1698 by Emperor Peter I of Russia. His beard tax lasted until 1772 and was levied on a sliding scale based on a person's wealth.

Fur Was Banned as Early as 1337 ... Even for The Royal Household

A nearly 700-year-old rule prohibits wearing fur, even for members of the Royal household.

Early in the 14th century, the clothing became more extravagant, with garments lined with fur and made with more expensive cloth. With the spoils of war, knights and those of 'gentle blood' began purchasing these items and wearing such garments at the Royal court. This whole idea of '*keeping up with the Joneses*' persists in society today. Back then, it was considered more of an annoyance. When the lower classes started to imitate the clothing of those 'of gentle blood', it was felt that something had to be done about it.

King Edward III, who reigned from 1327 to 1377, passed a law preventing the wearing of fur as part of an outfit.

This early clothing law was designed to preserve and define wealth and social class distinctions and prevent the extravagant clothing styles that had become commonplace. This law banned anyone from wearing fur, including members of the Royal household. There were exceptions. Royal etiquette requires that on certain occasions, fur is worn, for example, at such State events as the State Opening of Parliament and coronations. On these occasions, fur was permitted to be worn but only by particular groups of people. Interestingly, this law is still active.

The punishment for unlawfully wearing fur was, and indeed still is, forfeiture of the fur and any further punishment *"at the King's Will."*

Illegal to Wear a Silk Nightcap to Bed If Your Annual Income Was Less Than £20

As part of his laws introduced to reinforce social and wealth divides, King Edward III's 1363 Statute of Diet and Apparel introduced harsh financial penalties for those who dared to wear garments considered to be above their social standing. Silk and fur were considered symbols of high wealth and status. So, it's no surprise they featured throughout the 1363 law. It heavily regulated the wearing of silk and the colour purple, which was designated for those of Royal blood.

The poor and servants' families were banned from wearing silk or fur. It decreed that handicraftsmen must not wear clothing valued over 40 shillings (£2), and their families were not permitted to wear silk, fur, or silk velvet. There was a scale of social standing which indicated precisely what each class could wear. This included merchants, gentlemen and the esquires, clergy and knights. It ordered that ploughmen must wear a blanket and a linen girdle.

According to this law, if anyone with an annual income less than £20 decided to wear a silk nightcap to bed, they would face three months imprisonment or a fine of £10 for each night worn. It also decreed that every person below the rank of a Lord was to wear a jacket covering his knees.

Women Not Permitted to Wear Make-up

Immediately after King Charles I had been executed, the Long Parliament, led by Cromwell, took over, and the country entered a time of Puritan harshness. There was a move away from anything considered fun like sporting activities, drinking alcohol, theatre and musical entertainment.

The Puritans believed that women should be strictly as nature had intended. Women were expected to dress in a long dark full-length dress with a white apron and wear their hair neatly tied behind a white headdress. They were expected not to dress in extravagant or colourful clothing or wear make-up. Whilst no specific laws prohibited wearing make-up, Puritan soldiers would nevertheless roam the streets and force any women they came across to remove make-up.

After several years of boring life, it's no small wonder that by the time the monarchy was restored in 1660 by King Charles II, society would have been rejoicing.

Illegal to Wear Trousers of 'Monstrous and Outrageous Greatness'

Throughout the Tudor times and onwards, King Henry VIII, Queen Mary I and Queen Elizabeth I passed laws to continue to control the styles of clothing throughout society. Queen Elizabeth took the matter very seriously and, on 6th May 1562, passed a law to put a stop to some of the 'outrageous' clothing styles at the time.

Throughout her reign, she issued eight separate proclamations about the excesses of clothing. These royal proclamations reinforced the clothing laws. It sought to remind people of the effect on the nation's wealth due to overspending on extravagant clothing. It notably considered the plight of several young gentlemen who had amassed significant debts due to excessive spending on their clothing and raised the fear that they might turn to crime to repay their debts. The real reason for this law was to ensure no 'inferior' person dressed above their station.

This 1562 law prohibited wearing shirts with "*outrageous double ruffs*" at the Royal court "*or in any other place within this realm.*" It also sought to reduce the wearing of extravagant hose (trousers) described as being of "*monstrous and outrageous greatness.*" It addressed the allowable length of swords and daggers "*crept alate into the realm.*" It applied penalties for tailors, hosiers or sword cutlers who made or sold such ridiculous items.

These laws were repealed during the reign of King James I.

Barristers Expressly Prohibited From Wearing Velvet Shoes and Double-Cuffed Shirts

Nowadays, if you attend any court across the UK, you will see how well turned-out our judiciary is, with judges and barristers resplendent in attire and personal appearance. It wasn't always this way, and during the Tudor reign of Queen Mary, attempts were made by the Inns of Court (the professional associations for barristers) to address the length of facial hair and unconventional clothing.

In 1555, the Inner Temple issued the following order, "if *any of the fellowship or company of this House ... Shall wear any beards above three weeks' growth, that then every such fellow that shall so wear his beard contrary to this order, for every time of offending to forfeit 20 shillings.*"

This was eventually extended to all houses, and it was later ordained that none of the companions under the degree of a Knight should wear their beards in such a fashion or they would be fined 40 shillings. This doubled each week thereafter for those who refused to shave.

The Middle Temple also sought to address clothing extravagances that had become commonplace. They passed an order that "*none of that society should wear great breeches in their hose, made after the Dutch, Spanish or Almain (German) fashion, or lawn upon their caps, or cut doublets.*" The penalty for breaking this rule was a fine of three shillings and four pence. For a second offence, the penalty was expulsion from the Middle Temple.

A year later, all of the Inns of Court passed orders that *"none of the companions, except knights or benchers, should wear in their doublets, or hose, any light colours, except scarlet and crimson; nor wear any upper velvet cap, or any scarf or wings in their gowns, white jerkins, buskins, or velvet shoes, double cuffs on their shirts, feathers or ribbons on their caps, on pain of forfeiting 3 shillings 4 pence and expulsion for the second offence."* Doublets were short, close-fitting padded jackets.

As bizarre as we may now view the regulation of dress codes, there's a good reason barristers attending court should not wear fancy dress or tracksuits and instead choose a more sombre style of clothing. The black robes currently worn by the judiciary date back to the reign of King Edward III, when in 1327, he declared that the legal profession must follow a dress code when attending the Royal court.

In 1635, a Royal decree was issued known as the Judges Rules. This regulated the attire of the judges. Following the death of King Charles II in 1685, the Bar began a period of mourning. Barristers' attire changed to the black mourning robes with pleated shoulders that we still see worn today. If you look closely at the back of a barrister's robe, you will also notice a piece of triangular cloth attached to the left shoulder. The origins of this accessory are no longer known, but there are two theories. The first is that it was originally a small money bag to deposit their fees. The second, and more plausible theory, is that it was a hood forming part of the mourning dress from the death of King Charles II.

An Impure Sword

This law goes back centuries. According to Anglo-Saxon law, a sword, implement of war or any other object that a person has used to kill another would then be classed as 'impure'.

The sword or item would no longer be considered pure until amends had been made for the death caused by it. Until then, the item was not to be used and should be set aside as a 'sacrifice'.

A cutler would refuse to accept the sword to repair it or for polishing unless they were first presented with a certificate stating that the item was now pure. If they did take in the tainted sword, it was felt its homicidal taint might harm them.

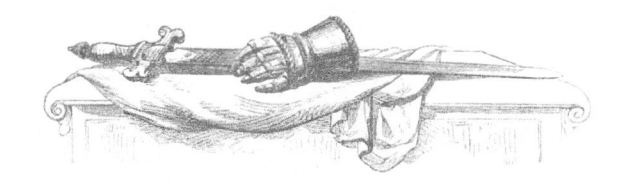

Chapter Four

Assault, Injury & Death

Hopefully history has taught us to be kind and do no harm to others. However, it is littered with some unconventional examples of where people have been unable to control their irritability or have acted out of paranoia.

In this chapter, we take a brief look at the changing face and levels of tolerance towards domestic abuse and the law preventing evil Bond villains wishing to take over the world by exploding a nuclear device in the capital.

In a nutshell, you can't kill a ghost, you can't kill another person, and you can't kill yourself.

Illegal to Kill a Ghostly Apparition

This story unfolds on the streets of Hammersmith on the outskirts of London. From December 1803, the local villagers reported multiple sightings of a ghost covered in a white burial shroud. Unfortunately, due to fear and mass hysteria, rumours became rife that the ghostly apparition was starting to attack people, especially in the vicinity of the Hammersmith churchyard.

The locals believed it was the ghost of a man who had died unpeacefully, and this was his punishment to walk the earth for all eternity. Such was the fear caused by these sightings that it scared the driver of a wagon. The driver ran off in fear for his life, leaving behind his eight horses and 16 passengers. A pregnant woman allegedly came into contact with the apparition, which caused her to faint. She was later reported to have died. The local community set up a neighbourhood watch group to look for the ghostly spectre.

It transpired that the ghostly apparition wasn't anything of the sort and was, in fact, a local bricklayer called Thomas Millwood who wore his white trade clothing late at night. He had previously been mistaken for a ghost due to his clothing. His relatives had even begged him not to wear such clothing late at night. Unfortunately, he ignored them.

Late on the evening of 3rd January 1804, Thomas Millwood left his house wearing his distinctive white linen trousers, a white flannel waistcoat, a white apron and white shoes. On this same night, one slightly drunk neighbourhood watchman, Francis Smith, took a shotgun with him.

As it happened, on this fateful night, Smith shot at what he claimed was a ghostly apparition coming toward him in the darkened street. Sadly, it was Thomas Millwood, the bricklayer. Smith went on trial at the Old Bailey for murder. In his defence, he stated that he genuinely believed Millwood was a ghostly apparition, and that's why he had shot him. The jury accepted this defence and found him guilty of the lesser offence of manslaughter. However, the judge sent them back to deliberate once again and either convict him of murder or acquit him entirely. They found him guilty of murder, and he was sentenced to death. Still, public sympathy later commuted this with a pardon from the Crown to one-year imprisonment.

Illegal to Cause a Nuclear Explosion

Believe it or not, it is illegal to cause a nuclear explosion in the UK. The law makers felt it was necessary to create a law to cover such an occurrence in case anyone was daft enough to consider making one.

A law was passed to ban nuclear weapons test explosions and other nuclear explosions. This makes it an offence to cause an explosion in the UK and any other country if you are a British national.

Should you inexplicably decide to cause a nuclear explosion, you have a defence. You must knowingly have caused the explosion, so an accidental one should be just fine.

Should the mood take you, please be advised that the local constabulary doesn't take too kindly to mushroom clouds drifting across the local bowling greens.

Six Feet Under

The expression "6 feet under" is a well-known euphemism for being dead and buried. It's based on the idea that people are buried in graves 6 feet deep. But is this actually the case? And if so, is there any legal foundation for this burial depth?

During the Norman times, most burials were conducted in relatively shallow pits. These were typically bath-shaped, just large enough to accommodate the corpse. Burial plots were often reused over and over because this increased the churches' income. So why did we change from shallow burial plots to deep graves?

For that reason, it's most likely that we have to look towards the 17th century and the outbreak of the plague or Black Death. Between the years 1665 and 1666, an estimated 100,000 plague victims (20% of the population) were in the capital. So many dead bodies piling up caused a public hygiene issue. A scheme was devised to bury them in mass graves called 'plague pits.' These were sometimes 20 feet deep. At the time, no-one knew that fleas spread the plague on rats. It was thought that deep burials would be better to prevent the risk of disease from spreading.

Such was the fear of the Black Death that the Lord Mayor of London issued an order with a long list of restrictions on how people were to travel and conduct themselves during the plague. It ordered that burials should occur during sunrise or sunset and that whilst relatives could attend the burial, friends and neighbours were not allowed. The key sentence within the Lord Mayor's directive was that "*all the graves shall be at least six feet deep.*"

These days, although the law states where a grave can be dug, for instance, it can't be close to water supplies or drains, there is no longer a legal requirement for a specified depth of a grave in the UK.

The reality is that many graves today are far deeper than 6 feet to accommodate the multiple coffins often stacked on top of each other in a single burial plot.

Dead Bodies Legally Required to be Buried in Wool Just to Stimulate the English Woollen Trade

Between 1665 and 1666, the country was going through a terrible time and was gripped with fear of the bubonic plague.

Most of the dead would be buried wearing linen shrouds. This was England's second biggest import, straight from France, which provided a third of our linen at the time.

Presumably, seeing a chance to capitalise on the rising death rate, in 1666, King Charles II assented to a law to help the English woollen industry. It was passed to ensure that all bodies were buried in a shroud made of woollen cloth. The law was brought in for the encouragement of the English woollen manufacturers and the prevention of the export of money to France to purchase French linen. The penalty for breaking this law was a £5 fine.

It appears that this law didn't go down too well at the time, with people expressing concern about changing from wool to linen. As a result, Parliament passed another law in 1677, setting stricter rules surrounding the burial in wool. It required that all burials be accompanied by sworn statements, with two witnesses, within eighty days from burial, affirming that a woollen shroud had been used.

It is estimated that this law stopped the import of around 23 million yards of French linen between 1679 and 1695. This equated to approximately £2.5 million, or in today's money, that would be about £359 million.

These laws remained on the statute books until they were repealed in 1814.

You Can Bury Your Relatives in The Garden

It's not just your cats, dogs, fish and hamsters that you can bury in your garden. You can also bury your relatives under the begonias in the garden.

This isn't as uncommon as you'd imagine. People just don't talk about it. Perhaps, the house where you live has a few bodies under the garden ... just something to think about when you're trying to sleep tonight.

ASSAULT, INJURY & DEATH 63

In 2021, there was a well-publicised case of a 61-year-old gentleman being buried in the garden of his three-bedroom house in Leeds, West Yorkshire. The gentleman had died after accidentally choking. His dying wish was to be buried in the garden of the house where he was born. Several weeks after his passing, the local vicar consecrated the ground. The house was later put up for sale.

A notice on the estate agent's particulars of sale stated, *"Please be aware this property is being sold by family members as part of a relative's estate. It was the deceased's wishes to be buried in the garden as he was born and died in the house. This wish has been carried out and the property will be sold as is."*

Residents living nearby spoke of their shock and surprise at this revelation. As bizarre as this sounds, it is legally possible to bury a loved one in your garden. This law was passed in 1880. It isn't as simple as dragging the corpse to the bottom of the garden in the dead of night, digging a hole and throwing it in. That sort of a scenario might get you a visit with a few enquiries from your local Constabulary.

On a side note, whilst you can get away with burying dear Uncle Albert under the flower bed, you can not cremate him in your garden. Cremations can only take place in a licensed crematorium.

Chapter Five
BEHAVIOUR

Over the centuries, different generations have looked upon each other with suspicion and confusion, as contemporary customs and behaviour changed. They say, '*There's nowt so queer as folk.*' This is very true, and as custodians of this planet and shepherds of all creatures thereupon, we must remember that our humble domesticated pets are probably looking at us and thinking this very same thing.

In this chapter, we will examine some of our strange behaviours over the centuries for which laws have had to be passed, in some cases, to protect us from ourselves.

Be warned, if you are a woman, the law may not look favourably upon you, should you decide to be quarrelsome or argumentative with your neighbours ... you may find yourself being sold off for a pint of beer at the local inn.

No Abusive or Obscene Language in Libraries

I would hope this is common sense in any case to my readers, but for those given to moments of madness, please remember, that it is an offence to use abusive or obscene language in a library.

You wouldn't just be on the receiving end of a stern look, a hush and a retort of "*Quiet in the library!*" You could receive a fine. It is an offence in England and Wales for any person to annoy or disturb others in the library by behaving in a disorderly manner or using violent, abusive, or obscene language, betting or gambling. It is also an offence to remain in the library after the "*library's closing now*" warning. The punishment for such poor behaviour in the library is a fine of up to 40 shillings.

This law is still in force but the relevant sections covering offences in public libraries have since been repealed. Not to worry though, for those sensitive to the use of obscene language or the calls of "*Bogies*" by television presenters Dick and Dom, other laws exist to provide suitable punishments for such transgressions.

Illegal to Behave in a Disorderly Manner in a Public Library

We have always taken our libraries seriously, as repositories of knowledge for all generations. Our oldest surviving library in Britain can be found at the back of Victoria train station in Manchester. It's Chetham's Library, founded in 1653. The library is still in use today.

The modern-day public libraries that we find in cities, towns and villages across the UK were brought about with a law passed in 1850. This enabled local boroughs to establish their own free public libraries providing free access for all to information and literature. The first of these modern-day public access libraries was The Royal Museum & Public Library (now the Salford Museum and Art Gallery), which opened in November 1850.

Being open to 'all', the libraries must have, at times, attracted some rather undesirable behaviour which required laws to be passed to put a stop to it. There is a specific offence for a person to behave in a disorderly manner "*to the annoyance or disturbance of any person.*" This law is still live today. The original fine for being 'annoying' was forty shillings. Nowadays, you're more likely just to be asked to leave the library.

Illegal to Sound a Gong in Morecambe & Heysham

We have some deliciously outdated bylaws in Lancashire. One such council bylaw that had been in force in Morecambe and

Heysham since 1907 stated that ringing a bell, sounding a gong or playing the trumpet, or "*any other noisy instrument*" was prohibited in public along the promenade.

I'm not sure whether this bylaw was brought in just to reduce noise or to dissuade visiting Morris Dancers or wannabe Punch & Judy shows on the promenade. The bylaws were last updated in 1978. According to the Lancaster City Council, these bylaws were revoked on 8th December 2006.

The Swear Box

This one is for any potty-mouthed readers (you know who you are!)

In 1650, one year after the execution of King Charles I, Parliament passed a law for '*the better preventing of profane swearing and cursing*' in an attempt to kerb the use of profanity, swearing and cursing.

Offenders were punished depending upon their social standing. A Lord would be fined 30 shillings; a Baronet or Knight 20 shillings; an Esquire 10 shillings; a simple gentleman was to pay 6 shillings and 8 pence, and people of 'inferior quality' were fined 3 shillings and 4 pence. These fines were doubled for a second offence. For a 10th offence, the offender, irrespective of their social status, would be adjudged a 'Common Swearer or Curser'.

A failure to pay the fines would result in the offender being publicly displayed in the village stocks for three hours, or if they were under 12 years old, they would receive a whipping. If none of this stopped the continual swearing, the offender would have all of their possessions seized and sold.

These days, a person is only guilty of swearing in public if it is done *"within the hearing or sight of a person likely to be caused harassment, alarm or distress thereby."*

Cutting Flowers in The Local Park

Perhaps you walked around your local park and saw a lovely bush in glorious bloom and considered taking a small cutting to grow in your garden. Maybe you may have seen hundreds of daffodils and thought a few wouldn't go amiss on your windowsill, or perhaps a small bunch of bluebells.

Most will have considered that at some point. This is precisely what happened in March 2011 when a couple were approached and told off by police in Whitecliffe Park in Poole, Dorset. What had happened was that their three girls, aged 10, 6 and 4 years old, had been seen picking some daffodils in their local park. This had been reported to the police who attended. Unfortunately, the caller had apparently embellished the story, which prompted the police to attend. As it happened, the young girls had only picked a few daffodils out of many hundreds. The police provided words of advice, and the family were allowed to go on their way. On Mother's Day in 2017, there was a similar occurrence in Mansfield, Nottinghamshire. On this occasion, a father had taken his two young daughters, aged 10 and 5, to pick some daffodils from a grassed area at the roadside. They were seen by a police officer who seized the bunch of 27 daffodils that the young girls had gathered. Again, the officer provided words of advice.

The law makes it an offence to:

- Uproot any wild plant without permission from the landowner or occupier;
- Pick flowers from a special conservation site or reserve, including National Trust properties;
- Pick any flower that is considered to be 'highly threatened';
- Pick with the intention to sell or advertise to sell bluebells or tree lungwort

Picking any part of the plant is legal so long as you don't uproot the entire plant. You can also pick bluebells, provided that you don't sell them.

It is also illegal to pick cultivated flowers in public parks or gardens and plants and flowers growing on land maintained by the council. This includes, for example, roundabouts and grass verges on the roadside. It would be an offence of theft if you picked flowers that a private organisation or individual had cultivated. To frighten you even more, if you pick any rare or endangered plants, you could face up to six months imprisonment and a maximum fine of £5,000.

Illegal for Women to Argue & Quarrel

As far back as mediaeval times, it was considered wrong to use offensive or abusive speech in public. This became known as 'scolding' and became a crime in 1350. Most of the earlier cases of this crime were brought against women who were considered argumentative and quarrelsome towards their neighbours.

A 'common scold' was a nuisance to the general public. It was generally considered to be any troublesome or angry person who constantly chastised, argued and quarrelled with their neighbours.

In 1585, Queen Elizabeth I passed a law which provided the offence of being a 'common scold'. This made it illegal to cause a nuisance with abusive or argumentative language or openly quarrelling with others. The majority of those charged with this offence were troublesome women.

Women found to be common scolds could be imprisoned, but in most cases, a humiliating punishment was preferred. Several methods were available. These included being forced to wear the scold's bridle in public, being dragged around town on a scold's cart, dunked in a nearby river or pond on a ducking stool, or placed into the village stocks.

The scold's bridle was a metal cage or mask fitted around the offender's head. It had a mouthpiece fitted into the woman's mouth to prevent her from continuing her 'quarrelsome' ways. Sometimes this mouthpiece was a bolt or spike which held the tongue up against the roof of the mouth, causing discomfort should the wearer choose to excessively wag her tongue in anger. In other bridles, the mouthpiece was a sharp piece of metal with a serrated edge which would cause lacerations to the wearer's tongue if they tried to speak.

Records show that a Martha Farrant of Salford (now in Greater Manchester) was once ordered to 'put' on 'the bridle' and wear it for an hour. The last recorded use of the scold's bridle was as late as 1856, when it was used on a woman in Bolton-le-Moors, Lancashire.

The scold's cart would be just as humiliating, where the scolding woman would have her head shaved, then be tied to a cart and dragged around her local village or town for all to see. The ducking stool was the most common form of punishment for a quarrelsome woman. Like the scold's bridle, this practice continued into the 19th century.

At one time, the ducking stool could be found in most villages as a common method of deterrence and public humiliation for offenders. The offender would be forced to sit in the chair, their arms would be fastened to it, and the chair would be dunked into the water repeatedly. It seems a bit bizarre, considering this is the sort of thing we now watch on Ninja Warrior or Japanese game shows.

The last recorded use of the ducking stool occurred in Leominster in 1809. This was Jenny Pipes, who was considered to be a "notorious" scold from Leominster. Unhappy with her husband, she decided to make some very unpleasant comments about him in public. The local magistrate didn't take kindly to this and chose to make an example of her. Mrs Pipes was dragged through the streets on a scold's cart and taken to the nearby River Kenwater. Unfortunately for her, the route taken went right passed her house, with her neighbours all watching in amazement. People travelled from afar to watch this public spectacle as the local ducking stool hadn't been used for years.

Quarrelsome women need no longer fear because this law was finally repealed in 1967.

Death For Heretics and Blasphemy

In 1647, a law was passed declaring that Wednesday, 10th March 1647, would be a day of Public Humiliation where people should seek God's *"direction and assistance"* to put a stop to and prevent any further heresy and blasphemy.

This didn't seem to work. So, the following year, Parliament passed another law making it an offence for anyone to preach, teach, write or publish *"that there is no God, or that God is not present in all places."* This law went on extensively to state that it was illegal for people to deny almost every book of holy scripture. A person suspected of this offence would be committed to prison without bail. In prison, the offender was given a chance to admit the error of his ways.

If he refused to admit the error of his ways, he would remain in prison until two people could be found to take responsibility for his future actions and he was bound over never again to commit such errors. If he continually committed the offence, he was put to death.

Such laws in today's multi-faith society would be considered unthinkable.

Illegal to Even Imagine The Abolition of The Monarchy

I imagine this law will raise a few eyebrows, not so much for what it deals with but more to do with the restraint it places on a person's words and also their thoughts. Believe it or not, a law passed in 1848, which is still a crime today, makes it an offence to call for the abolition of the monarchy. The law was passed during the early years of the reign of Queen Victoria.

This law makes it an offence to even "*imagine*" overthrowing or abolishing the Crown. This is a very serious criminal offence for which the penalty is to be "*transported beyond the seas for the term of his or her natural life.*" When you get into the nitty-gritty of the law, essentially, it deals with promoting the abolition of the monarchy in print, for example, in newspapers and most likely online.

Since transporting criminals overseas was abolished in 1868, the sentence would now be life imprisonment.

Interestingly, the last prosecution under this law was in 1883.

There is No Offence of Urinating in Public

There is no actual offence of urinating in a public place. However, before you drop your trousers and urinate on the flower beds in the local park, I better point out that you can't get off Scot-free.

The Law Commission has pointed out that there is no general offence of urinating in a public place. However, such an activity would be covered by other laws. Local authorities are allowed to create their own bylaws, making public urination an offence. Urinating in public can also be considered an offence of Public Order. You could receive a fine of £50 or £80.

There is also a popular myth that pregnant women are legally permitted to urinate anywhere they wish, including into a police constable's helmet. This is false. No such law exists nor is believed to have ever existed.

Hard Labour & Whipped For Defacing Library Books

In the UK, over the centuries, various laws have been passed to address people causing damage to property. A law passed in 1861 made it an offence to damage books and artwork.

The penalty for being found guilty was imprisonment, with or without hard labour. Any boys aged under sixteen could also face a whipping. Interestingly, it was this offence for which the playwright Joe Orton and his partner Kenneth Halliwell were found guilty and imprisoned in 1962.

Orton and Halliwell met and fell in love when they both attended RADA. In 1959, they moved into a bed-sit flat in the London borough of Islington. It was then that their latest 'collage' project had begun in earnest. Over three years, they removed illustrations from hundreds of art books shelved at their local Islington Library. They wallpapered their room with these torn-out book images. Their project also extended to creating new amusing dust jackets for other books made from the doctored scraps of artwork they had previously torn. These new alternative dust covers were quietly replaced on the library shelves for unsuspecting browsers to discover.

An Offence to Sell Your Wife

In 2003, a 35-year-old man from Wrexham in Wales, decided to advertise his wife for sale on the auction website eBay. In his sales pitch, he noted, "*The chassis is in excellent order for the mileage, and warranty given at extra cost.*" This happened again in 2016 when a man from Wakefield, Yorkshire, put his "*Used Wife*" up for sale on the same auction site. He wrote. "*Not new has been used but still got some good miles left in her ... Reason for selling ... feel like there HAS to someone out there that is more deserving of her [than] me (oh dear god please let there be).*" He amassed 57 bids for his wife, with the highest bidder offering to pay £65,888 before eBay eventually removed the post. Whilst this was all very tongue-in-cheek and neither wife was actually sold, there have been multiple times throughout our history when husbands have sold their wives.

The majority of wife sales were carried out in local market squares. The husband would often parade his wife around the market square, leading her around with a halter made of rope or ribbon around her neck or waist. She would be publicly auctioned to the highest bidder. Wives were sold for varying amounts. This sometimes increased if they came with children. One of the highest amounts paid is recorded as £150. On other occasions, wives were sold for nothing more than a simple glass of ale at the local inn.

The sales weren't considered legal, but everyone turned a blind eye to them. It is important also to note that the sales weren't 'forcible'. By that, I mean that they depended on the wife's consent. Sales were advertised in advance of the auction through the local newspaper or on local noticeboards. In fact, in many cases, the sales were pre-arranged between seller and purchaser, and the sale in public was more of an act to convince the local community of the arrangement.

There are earlier accounts of wife selling. For instance, an account exists from 1302 of a man who *"granted his wife by deed to another man."* By the early 18th century, instances of wife selling started to be reported in popular newspapers. One such report can be found in The Annual Register in August 1733. The article states, *"Three men and three women, went*

to the Bell Inn in Edgbaston Street, Birmingham, and made the following entry in the toll book which is kept there: - Samuel Whitehouse, of the parish of Willenhall, in the county of Stafford, sold his wife, Mary Whitehouse, in the open market, to Thomas Griffiths, of Birmingham. Value, one guinea. To take her with all her faults."

In 1740, we saw probably the most high-profile case of wife selling, that of Henry Brydges, 2nd Duke of Chandos. He was reported to have purchased his second wife from a local ostler (stable hand). In another case, in 1790, a man in Ninfield, East Sussex, sold his wife for half a pint of gin at the local village inn. He later changed his mind and repurchased her. On 18th July 1797, even The Times newspaper reported on wife selling. In this case, a local butcher had *"exposed his wife to sale in Smithfield Market, near the Ram Inn, with a halter about her neck, and one about her waist which tied her to a railing."* The wife's new 'owner' was a local hog driver who paid the sum of three guineas and a crown. A year later, a wife was sold for 7 shillings and eight pots of beer in Brighton.

In 1855, another wife was sold in Chipping Norton in the Cotswolds for the generous amount of £25. I say 'generous' because the going rate seems to have been around 2-3 shillings. By this time, Victorian values had started to trickle through society and wife selling was seen as disrespectful. So, on this occasion, the sale didn't go according to plan. The locals had other ideas and subjected the purchaser and his new wife to three nights of 'rough music'. This was a form of punishment where the offenders would be subjected to irritating noises and the singing of rude songs. On the third night, they burned an effigy of the purchaser outside his house. He went back on his sale and offered money to her first husband to take her back. In 1865, a wife was sold for the sum of £100. Along with the sale went the two children, which cost the purchaser an additional £25 each.

Wife selling was, thankfully, slowly becoming a dying practice. Although records indicate, that they were still occurring, albeit seldomly. In 1913, a woman gave evidence in a Leeds police court that her husband had sold her to one of his work colleagues for £1. The practice itself was illegal. You can't just sell your wife, even if she did agree. Several wife sales did result in prosecution.

Illegal to be Drunk and in Charge of a Horse, Cattle or a Cow

It is an offence for *'Every person who is drunk while in charge on any highway or other public place of any carriage, horse, cattle, or steam engine.'* Those who fell foul of this law could be liable for a fine of up to 40 shillings or a month in prison.

This is somewhat unsurprising considering that a male adult bull weighs more than several modern-day cars. It can cause considerable damage when ridden by a drunken farmer!

Chapter Six

COURTS

It wasn't always the accused that would find themselves in the dock of a court. Often, jury members would be treated with more contempt than the accused. They would find themselves fined or imprisoned alongside the defendant for refusing to agree with the judges.

Through an interpretation of an old law from 1361, we'll see that magistrates are, even now, legally compelled to bind over every person, even if they're already of good behaviour.

There's no place to hide in this chapter. In case you don't hear your name being called by a court, you may end up paying a heavy fine.

Magistrates Are Legally Required to Bind Over Every Person of Good Behaviour

The Justices of The Peace Act (1361), which is still in force today, missed out a very important word, "*not*." This law, passed during the reign of King Edward III, intended to deal with the various problems arising from mass unemployment at the time.

During his reign, the King led the English army to a famous victory at Crécy in France and captured Calais. Unfortunately, things took a turn for the worse, and the French won back most of the territory the English had conquered. The returning soldiers were no longer needed, nor did they have any jobs to return to. This created mass unemployment and what was considered to be laziness. Many of the returning soldiers were deemed to have become "*pillors and robbers*." Those were the words used in the 1361 Act. The law provides Justices of The Peace (magistrates) with the power to "*restrain...pursue, arrest...and chastise*" any "*offenders, rioters, and all other barators*" and imprison, fine or deal with them using their own discretion.

The problem is that the law was written in Norman French and doesn't translate very well.

It has been translated as, "*to take all them that be of good fame, where they shall be found, sufficient surety and mainprise of their good behaviour towards the King and his people, and the other duly to punish.*" The word 'not' was left out. It should say, "*to take all them that be not of good fame.*" Essentially, the law requires all those brought before magistrates, who are of good behaviour, to be bound over.

As recently as 1978, an amendment to the law was put forward in the House of Commons but this was voted down in Parliament. So the wording of the original 1361 law still stands to this day.

Juries Could Be Fined or Imprisoned If The Judge Wasn't Happy With Their Decision

The right to trial by jury is something that we take for granted these days. It came about in 1215 at Runnymede when rebellious land barons forced King John to agree to a Charter of liberties, later known as the Magna Carta.

These days, doing jury service is seen as a valuable civic duty. You decide the verdict with your fellow jurors in the comfort of the court building jury room, regularly supplied with refreshments, and there are no time pressures. It is the jury who decide whether a person is guilty or not guilty. It wasn't always that way. During the 16th century, juries would often be fined or imprisoned if they disagreed with the 'advice' of the judge regarding the verdict.

In 1667, the Lord Chief Justice Kelynge attracted many complaints for fining and imprisoning jurors if their verdicts were different to the advice of the court.

On 14th August 1670, William Penn and William Mead attended their Quaker meeting house in Gracechurch Street, London. They noticed that the authorities had padlocked the doors. They chose to address the crowd of approximately three hundred, preaching to them in the street. This was in contravention of a recently passed law, which banned gatherings of more than five people for worship in a public place. Penn and Mead were arrested for unlawful assembly and preaching. Both men appeared at the Old Bailey in London on 1st September 1670 for a five-day trial.

When Penn began shouting that their rights were being denied under the conventions set out in the Magna Carta, they were both thrown into the dungeon, away from the earshot of the court. The whole court case was a complete shambles. The members of the jury believed both Penn and Mead to be innocent. The court was not happy and threatened the jury that if they didn't find Penn and Mead guilty, they would themselves would be imprisoned. The judge locked the jury away for the night without food, drink, fire, and tobacco. Each time they returned a verdict of not guilty, the judge became angry and sent them back to reconsider.

Eventually, the judge told them off for not following the advice of the court. He fined each juror 40 marks, and they were sent to Newgate prison until they paid their fines.

Judge Sir John Vaughan stated that a jury must be independent, and a judge "*may try to open the eyes of the jurors, but not lead them by the nose.*" He found that the imprisonment of the jury was not legal and contrary to the Magna Carta. This became a landmark ruling in English law, once and for all establishing the jury's independence. It has since become known as Bushel's Case (named after one of the jurors).

Following this, all of the jurors were released from prison.

Juries Who Took Too Long to Agree a Verdict Were Carried Around in Carts

Thankfully, a judge is no longer permitted to force a jury to return a verdict. If the jury can't agree on a verdict, then after a while, the jury will be sent home. This is known as a 'hung jury'. These days, judges are always very careful to ensure that the jury never feels under time pressure to reach a verdict.

However, it hasn't always been that way. In past centuries, the judges would travel around, judging cases at various courts in different towns within their area. It was accepted practice that a judge didn't need to wait for the jury's verdict before the end of their court sittings. Instead, the jury was detained and carried around in a cart from town to town, until they had reached their verdict.

Juries Could Be Kept Locked Away Without Food, Drink, Warmth or Light Until They Reached a Unanimous Verdict

At the end of a court case, the jury will retire to decide whether a person is guilty or not guilty. A jury's decision should be based on the evidence before them in court. They will decide what points of law have been proved and whether there is sufficient evidence to convict a person beyond all reasonable doubt.

A judge will always first seek a unanimous verdict. This is a verdict upon which all of the twelve jury members agree. These days, members of the jury are treated well, they are provided refreshments and, in most cases, permitted to leave the court at the end of each day. However, this wasn't always the case. In years gone by, they were effectively imprisoned by the courts for the duration of the trial. This was done to prevent anyone interfering with the trial.

Judges didn't have to wait for the jury to return their unanimous verdict. If the jury were taking too long, the judge would simply leave and travel around the area, taking the jury members with him, in a cart, to the next town, where he would proceed to hear other cases. Presumably, the jury members then had to make their own way back to their homes, however far away that might have been. Eventually, this practice also stopped and was replaced with judges locking the jury away without any food, drink, warmth or light until such a time as they reached a unanimous verdict.

This practice was finally abolished in 1870, after which jurors were allowed to have fire and refreshments but at their own expense.

As recently as 1908, a jury who said that they were unable to reach a unanimous verdict, were told by the judge that they would be locked up for two hours. By unanimous verdict, they found the prisoner guilty.

Submission Shaming

During the reign of King James I, we find the curious case of Mylward v Weldon in 1596, in which the son of one of the litigants submitted a 120-page document to the court. The court felt that the submission could be made in just 16 pages. The Lord Keeper of the Great Seal was so outraged by this, that he promptly imprisoned Richard Mylward in the notorious debtor's prison, the Fleet, until he paid the sum of £10 to the Crown and a further sum to the defendant for causing him to read his lengthy document.

The Lord Keeper also ordered that a hole should be cut in the middle of the large document and for the pages to be hung around Mylward's head. He was then led around Westminster Hall and shown to all three courts within the Hall, before being returned to the Fleet prison.

Things were so much simpler then. These days, parading a lawyer around with excessive documents over his head is considered unnecessary.

The Lawless Court

A curious type of court existed in ancient times and is believed to have continued until the beginning of the twentieth century.

This was the 'Lawless Court', also known as the 'Whispering Court' in Rochford, Essex.

It is believed the first sitting of this ancient court was sometime before 1661, being called by the Lord of the Manor of King's Hill. One morning, he was awoken by the crowing of a local cockerel. Coincidentally, he noticed that some of his servants were plotting his murder as he awoke. He convicted them of treason and spared his sentence of forfeiture of their lands in return for what he called a shameless service. He declared that each year on the first Wednesday morning after Michaelmas Day, the local tenants from the manor would be called to assemble in the place where he discovered their plot to kill him. On this occasion each year, the Lord's Steward would kindly remind the tenants of the need to assemble. However, he would do this by whispering their names as quietly as possible.

Any tenants who failed to answer when their name was whispered would be fined double their rents for each hour they failed to respond to their name. The tenants were then required to remain assembled at that location until the cockerel crowed three times, at which point they were dismissed from the court.

Another peculiarity of this court was the fact that no candles were permitted. The court had to be lit by natural light. The use of ink was also forbidden, so the names of those who had answered were written down with a piece of charcoal in the dark.

This bizarre court continued, as a tradition, each year without fail until the late 19th century, after which it met periodically until the early 20th century.

It is believed that the tenants became so fed up with this annual tradition of waking up in the middle of the night and standing for hours in a damp room, that many instead chose to pay double rent the following morning. And as time went on, a local man was even employed to make the noise of a cockerel crowing to bring the court proceedings to a swift close.

Pardoned From The Death Sentence on a Technicality

During the 19th century, it was common practice for those who had received the death sentence to be buried within the grounds of the prison. At the same time, it was also necessary, when passing a sentence, for the judge to provide instructions as to what should happen to the body after the death sentence has been carried out.

In 1840, in the city of Cork, Ireland, the court heard the case of R v Hartnett and Casey. In this case, the judge forgot to provide instructions that the bodies of the deceased should be buried within the grounds of the prison. Upon realising his mistake, a couple of days later, the judge corrected his error and, in open court, directed that Hartnett and Casey's bodies should be buried within the grounds of the prison. However, as required by law, he neglected to do this in the hearing and presence of both defendants. The matter was then brought before the appeal judges. Six of the ten appeal judges agreed that this had made the sentence of death illegal. They decided that the judgement should be reversed. Both defendants were pardoned and walked free.

Chapter Seven
Death & Execution

We're all familiar with the name Guy Fawkes and the Gunpowder Plot. After suffering an excruciating ordeal on the rack, he was put to death in the only way possible for those convicted of high treason: hanged, drawn and quartered. This was a particularly gruesome method of execution, devised to create as much fear as possible right to the point of death.

Over the centuries, our ancestors have developed some elaborate methods of execution. Executions were a very public affair, from beheading for commoners to the more mundane commonplace hangings in the town square.

Unsurprisingly much of this chapter is devoted to King Henry VIII. It seemed to be his favourite pastime. We look at the different methods of execution used for commoners and noblemen. We also see how gender played a significant role in deciding the mode of execution.

Hanged, Drawn and Quartered

Those found guilty of treason would be held in isolation for a while, usually in the Tower of London, to increase their levels of fear and anxiety. They would often be allowed to see some of the instruments of their torture and execution before death. They would also be forced to watch the execution of other traitors to give them a taste of what's in store for them.

On the day of their execution, they would be stripped to the waist and tied either to the back of a horse or placed on a wooden cart. They would then be taken (drawn) to the executioner's scaffolding and forced to climb it. The King's commission would be read aloud in front of the large crowds waiting to witness this gruesome spectacle; the public would be asked to move back from the scaffold. The prisoner would be allowed to give a final address to the crowd. This is the famous '*Any last words?*' Most of the time, these would be admissions of guilt or some act of repentance, possibly the Lord's prayer.

Their arms were bound in front of them, and they were hanged for a short period to cause suffering and the feeling of asphyxiation. Most prisoners would wish they had died at this point, but unfortunately, their suffering was only starting. They were immediately cut down. A large cross would be cut in their stomach, and their bowels would be ripped out and thrown into a bonfire to burn before their eyes. At the same time, their testicles would be cut off. His heart would then be removed. Following death, his head would be cut off, and his body would be chopped into four pieces (quartered).

Sometimes, the executioner was not as skilled in the art as they should have been, and things didn't always go smoothly. At the execution of Richard Gwyn on 15th October 1584, the executioner did an appalling job of disembowelment. He had to remove the bowel piece by piece through a small hole in Gwyn's stomach.

Following the quartering, the severed head would be placed on a spike and displayed on London Bridge. This was one of the main routes to enter the City of London.

Interestingly, beheading for high treason was not abolished until 1973.

Beheading For Noble Traitors

Beheadings for noble people were carried out on Tower Hill, on the higher ground next to the Tower of London moat. The last person to be executed at Tower Hill was Simon Fraser, 11th Lord Lovat, beheaded for treason on 9th April 1747. Thousands of people would flock from miles around to attend these gruesome public events. The executioner would usually hold the severed head high and shout, "*Behold the head of [name of the executed], a traitor.*" Interestingly, these words were not spoken at the execution of King Charles I.

Whilst it was considered the swiftest and most painless method of execution, it didn't always go according to plan. There are still debates about whether the brain remains functional shortly after death. Eye witness accounts show that after the executioner severed Anne Boleyn's head with a single strike of his sword, her lips continued to move for several seconds in silent prayer.

One well-known botched beheading was that of Thomas Cromwell, who was executed on Tower Hill on 28th July 1540. Some sources have indicated that it took up to 3 blows of the axe by an executioner who is described as ragged, butcherly, ungoodly and a miser. Some accounts report that two executioners had to be involved and were chopping away at Cromwell's neck and head for nearly half an hour.

Finally, this brings us to the most unusual story of the execution of James Scott, 1st Duke of Monmouth. He was also the eldest son of King Charles II. Following the death of King Charles II in February 1685, the Crown passed to King James II. James Scott, being illegitimate, was ineligible as an heir to the throne. He tried to overthrow James II. The King had enough and ordered Monmouth' arrest. He was sentenced for treason. On 15th July 1685, Monmouth was led up to Tower Hill, where he was met by the famous executioner Jack Ketch. After inflicting between five and eight blows with his axe, during which it is said Monmouth tried to rise from the executioner's block, Monmouth's head had to be severed from his twitching body with the extra use of a knife. According to legend, following his execution, it was quickly realised that there was no official portrait of the Duke of Monmouth, as was tradition. So, his body was quickly dug up, his head stitched back on, and his portrait was painted in just a few hours before being just as quickly buried in the Church of St. Peter ad Vincula in the Tower of London.

Beheading For Commoners

Beheadings for commoners were a very different affair from that of noblemen. Noblemen were often beheaded on Tower Hill with an axeman, placing their heads on the chopping block. The beheading of commoners was often a very botched job.

Those sentenced to death by beheading were advised to tip the public executioner in advance. It was hoped this would encourage them to do a swift and efficient job, hopefully killing the victim in one clean blow. This did not always happen. The notorious public executioner, Jack Ketch, was well known for his botched executions. One such case occurred on 21st July 1683 at Lincoln's Inn Fields, after Lord William Russell had been convicted of attempting to kill King Charles II. Lord Russell had paid the executioner in advance, hoping he would make the execution swift and painless. Jack Ketch did such a bad job that, after the axe hit the side of Russell's head, Russell looked up at him and said, "*You dog, did I give you ten guineas to use me so inhumanely?*" It took him a further three axe blows to separate the head from the body, during which the watching crowd jeered Ketch. Ketch himself was sent to prison in 1686 for insulting a Sheriff. His assistant, Paskah Rose, became the public executioner in Ketch's absence. A few months later, Rose was also convicted and then hanged at Tyburn, leading to Ketch's reinstatement.

We often think of the guillotine as a French invention. Before it was introduced to France, an early form of the guillotine was in use in England. It was known as the '*Halifax Gibbet*'.

There was a peculiar custom surrounding the use of the Gibbet. It gave offenders a second chance. If an offender were fast enough to withdraw their head from the Gibbet in time to avoid the falling blade, they would be released if they left the town and never returned. On 29th January 1623, this did happen. The offender, John Lacy, managed to withdraw his head in time and left Halifax. Unfortunately for him, he returned seven years later, wrongly believing that he would have been pardoned in the meantime. He wasn't. He was re-arrested and taken back to the Gibbet. Sadly, the years had not been kind to Lacy. This second time around, he wasn't as fast as he once was. For him, there was no escaping the executioner a second time.

Women Were Drowned or Burned Alive

Our ancestors considered it too indecent to hang, draw and quarter women. Instead, they were either drowned or were dragged to the gallows, hanged and burned.

During the Middle Ages, women who stole were referred to as 'She-thieves' and were usually put to death by drowning.

DEATH & EXECUTION

The sentence of drowning the guilty was finally abolished in England in 1623 during the reign of King James I.

With drowning now off the books, what other method could still be used to execute women? Burning at the stake, of course! Burning was a legally prescribed punishment for women guilty of high and petty treason.

During the early burnings, prisoners would still be alive to suffer the whole ordeal. Later, they would be hanged or strangled by the executioner and then burned. In the reign of Queen Mary I, women were stripped naked, and a small bag of gunpowder was placed around their necks. This would eventually explode in the fire, quickening the prisoner's death as an act of mercy.

There were three distinctly different methods of burning women. One method saw bundles of sticks piled around a central wooden stake. The prisoner would be bound to the stake with iron chains. This was the preferred method, being the most theatrical. It satisfied the crowds of onlookers, watching the slow suffering and hearing the screams and agonising gurgles. It also provided the most suffering as it took a while for the flames to reach the prisoner's head; all the time, the rest of her body was burned. Another method saw the wooden sticks piled high around the central stake. This sped up the burning and death, with the flames quickly consuming the whole body whilst the smoke and hot fumes filled her lungs. The hot air would cause their trachea to swell, leading to asphyxia and death within minutes. The prisoner's suffering would be hidden behind a curtain of flames, but their screams could still be overheard. A third method, seldom used, saw the prisoner tied to the top of a tall ladder and slowly lowered over a burning fire pit.

The law also permitted the burning of children aged seven and above at the stake. In one such case, a 16-year-old Mary Troke was burned at the stake in Winchester on 18th March 1738, following her conviction for poisoning her mistress.

Catherine Murphy was the last woman in England to be burned at the stake. She was executed in 1789 for counterfeiting coins.

Hanging

Hanging was one of our most popular methods of execution from Saxon times right up to the mid-twentieth century. It certainly was one of the least gruesome methods of punishment. It is believed to have been introduced into England around the fifth century.

When William the Conqueror came to the throne, he favoured the earlier religious methods and ordered that hanging should be replaced by blinding and castration. It didn't disappear for too long, having been reintroduced during the reign of King

Henry I (1100-1135). It seems to have been the main mode of execution. This was certainly the case by the end of the eighteenth century.

From the early days, hanging used what was known as the 'Short drop' method. The criminal would have the noose placed around their neck, and they would stand on a stool or a ladder. This would then be pulled away quickly by rope, either by the executioner, the waiting crowds or even a horse. This led to very slow and painful strangulation until death. Regularly, friends and family of the prisoner would grab hold of their ankles to pull them down, to speed their strangulation and reduce their suffering.

In 1853, the previous 'Short drop' method was replaced with the 'Long drop', which saw the victim fall further, with the help of gravity, which snapped their neck. Death was instantaneous.

During the reign of Henry VIII, most public hangings were conducted at the gallows at Tyburn. Often, the important executions attracted crowds of up to 100,000 people. It became a very theatrical performance. The prisoners would be led up to the gallows, where the hangmen would uncoil a rope, throwing up the free end to an assistant who wrapped it around an upper beam. It would then be attached to a horse which was later whipped to quickly jerk forward, pulling the prisoner off their stand, to be left suspended in the air. They would writhe around in agony, kicking their legs whilst they slowly asphyxiated. This was known as *'dancing the Tyburn jig'*.

On 26th May 1868, the last public execution took place at Newgate. Michael Barrett was hanged for his involvement in a botched jailbreak at the Clerkenwell House of Detention. He planted explosives which subsequently went off and killed twelve bystanders, severely injuring many more. Following

Barrett's execution, all hangings were performed behind prison walls, out of view from the public.

A law passed in 1908 banned the hanging of children under the age of 16. This was raised to 18 years old in 1933. The last woman to be hanged in Britain was Ruth Ellis. She was hanged at HMP Holloway on 13th July 1955 for murder. The last people to be hanged in Britain were hanged on the same day, 13th August 1964. One was Peter Allen, hanged at Walton Prison in Liverpool. The other was Gwynne Evans, who was hanged at Strangeways Prison in Manchester. They were both hanged for the murder of van driver John West.

The death penalty for murder ceased to be used in 1965.

The Man They Could Not Hang

This is the story of John 'Babbacombe' Lee, famously known as 'the man they could not hang' after he was accused of murder and convicted on poor evidence. He went to work as a footman for Miss Emma Keyse at The Glen, Babbacombe, in Devon. Also working as servants at The Glen were Jane and Eliza Neck and the cook Elizabeth Harris.

In the early hours of 15th November 1884, Miss Keyse was found brutally murdered with her throat slit and three wounds to her head. There were signs that attempts had been made to burn her body. John Lee was the only suspect. He was charged and convicted because he was allegedly the only male in the house at the time of the murder. When the police arrested him, he had an inexplicable cut on his arm. Lee claimed that his own solicitor, Reginald Templar, had also been present in the house on the night of the murder. However, his pleas of innocence fell on deaf ears. Lee was insistent upon his innocence, and during his trial, Lee said to the judge, "*The reason I am so calm is that I trust in the Lord and he knows I am innocent.*" Despite this, he was sentenced to be executed by hanging and sent to Exeter prison to await this fateful day.

It finally arrived, and on 23rd February 1885, Lee made his way onto the platform, ready to be hanged. The noose was placed around his neck. The executioner, James Berry, tested the trapdoor and verified that it opened successfully. However, upon the first try, the trapdoor mechanism failed to work. This same thing happened another two times. On each occasion, the executioner confirmed that the trapdoor was functioning perfectly. You can only imagine the distress caused to the prisoner awaiting his impending doom. The medical officer refused to take part any further and walked off. The proceedings were stopped, and his execution was postponed. He was placed back in his cell. The then Home Secretary, then commuted the death sentence to a life sentence in prison.

In 1907, after 22 years in prison, John Lee was released and became known as '*Babbacombe Lee*', the man they could not hang.

Trial By Ordeal

Trial by ordeal was an ancient Saxon judicial practice to determine whether a person was innocent or guilty in the eyes of God. The trials, known as the judgement of God, required the accused to suffer an unpleasant and torturous process in the form of a dangerous 'trial'. The thinking behind the trial was that God would personally intervene with a miracle to help judge a person's innocence or guilt. Primarily, trials by ordeal consisted of Trial by hot iron, Trial by hot water, Trial by cold water, and Trial by blessed bread.

Most trials took place inside a church, except for the trial by cold water. In preparation for the trials, the accused person would fast for three days and then hear mass. A priest would always be present during the trial process.

Trial By Combat

Trial by combat, sometimes known as 'Ordeal by combat', was used when two parties had a dispute. This could be a dispute between two individuals or between a person and the State. The parties may elect, under certain circumstances, to designate a '*champion*' to undergo the ordeal on their behalf. This was separately referred to as '*Trial by champion*'. The Normans introduced this method of trial by ordeal in 1066.

It was considered that the victor had been chosen by God. The loser of the trial would be condemned as guilty and have to suffer whatever sentence followed.

The earliest known trial by combat occurred in 1077, between the two parties Wulfstan v. Walter.

Despite the abolition of trial by combat, in a typically British eccentric way, in 2002, Leon Humphreys, a Welshman, tried to challenge the Driver and Vehicle Licensing Agency (DVLA) to trial by combat. He refused to pay a penalty charge for a driving offence and appealed his fine. The matter was sent to Bury St. Edmunds Magistrates Court. Rather than pay the £25 fine, he proposed a dual using samurai swords, heavy hammers and Gurkha knives. The court rejected his request for this ancient mode of trial, and instead, he was fined £200, with an additional £100 for costs.

Trial By Hot Iron

Another method of trial by ordeal was '*Trial by Hot Iron*'. The accused would be required to pick up a searing hot iron weight, weighing one pound. The iron weight had been heated over a fire immediately before the accused grabbed it. They would then have to carry the weight a distance of nine feet. For more serious crimes like murder, the weight of the iron carried would be increased from 1lb to 3lbs. Once they let go of the iron weight, their hand would be bandaged up and unwrapped three days later. The accused would have been declared innocent if the wound had been cleanly healed. However, if the wound was blistered and festering, they would be declared guilty in the eyes of God. Interestingly, this trial by ordeal was usually taken by women.

Trial By Hot Water

'*Trial by Hot Water*' was a popular method of trial by ordeal. It was usually reserved for men and only for those considered to be common people.

It was first mentioned in records from the early sixth century. This ordeal would occur in the church in front of several high-profile attendees. They would first pray to God to reveal the truth.

Then, a large laundry cauldron had first to be filled with water. The water must be brought close to boiling temperature. A stone would be dropped into the cauldron. The accused would then plunge their hand into the boiling water and pick out the stone. Depending upon the severity of the offence for which the individual had been accused, they would either undertake a 'one-fold' ordeal or a 'three-fold' ordeal. For minor offences, a one-fold ordeal required the accused to plunge their hand into the cauldron up to the depth of their wrist. A three-fold ordeal would be prescribed for more serious crimes like treason or repeat offenders. This saw the accused plunging their arm into the cauldron up to the depth of their elbow.

The accused's hand or arm would then be bound tightly with a bandage and unwrapped and examined three days later. If the wound was cleanly healing, it was deemed that God had intervened, and the accused was pronounced innocent. However, if the wound was seen to be blistered or festering, the accused was condemned as a guilty man. We know from records that it wasn't just boiling water used in the cauldrons. Sometimes oil and lead were also used.

Trial By Cold Water

Another trial by ordeal usually reserved for commoners was *'Trial by Cold Water'*. The accused woman would first be required to drink some holy water. A rope would then be tied around her and knotted above her waist. She would then either be lowered into a pool of water or thrown in.

If the accused sank to the bottom, it was said that it was God's will, and the water had accepted her as pure. She was considered to be innocent of all charges. If she floated to the surface, it was said that the water had rejected her as impure and she was considered guilty. It is a myth that the innocent would sink and be left to drown. This was not usually the case. A rope was tied around their body to enable them to be retrieved following the judgement.

Trial by cold water was the method often used during the infamous witch trials conducted between the 15th and 17th centuries.

Trial By Fire

A method of trial by ordeal was the '*Trial by Fire*', sometimes known as 'Fire ordeal'. It was generally confined to those of a higher social status. The accused person would be forced to walk, blindfolded and barefooted, for a distance of around 9 feet (2.7 metres) or a set number of paces. That makes it sound like a school sports day race. It wasn't. On that set path they had to walk, nine red-hot ploughshares were laid out lengthwise at unequal distances. This prevented the accused from guessing where the ploughshares were placed and being able to avoid them.

If the accused escaped unhurt, they would be judged innocent. If they sustained any injury, the wounds would be bandaged and examined after the passage of three days. If the wounds had healed, it was considered that God had intervened to pronounce that the individual was innocent. However, if, as was more likely, the third-degree burns were festering, the accused would be condemned as guilty.

Trial by fire was still practised in England during the reign of King John (1199-1216).

Trial By Blessed Bread

Trial by Blessed Bread was a superstitious Saxon trial by ordeal. The thought behind this was that the guilty party would purge themselves by eating a piece of barley bread whilst a priest prayed that they would choke on the bread if they lied. It was felt that the bread would poison the accused or they would choke on it if they lied when questions were put to them. This particular trial by ordeal was only taken by priests.

Lex Talionis

Lex talionis is one of the oldest types of law and Latin for *'the law of retaliation'*. It primarily concerns revenge, believing that tit-for-tat is an acceptable response if a person has been wronged. It is essentially a case of doing unto others what they have done unto you, whereby the punishments resemble the offence committed both in type and severity.

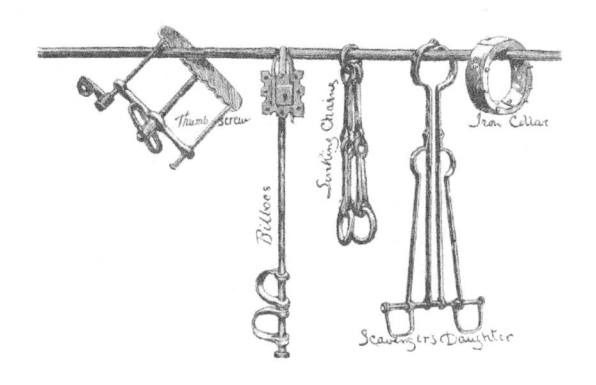

Lawful to Boil a Man Alive

Those sentenced to be executed by being boiled alive in a drum of boiling liquid would first be manacled in chains and strung up through a series of pulleys. They would then be dangled from a gibbet over a drum of boiling liquid. This could either be water, boiling oil or hot tar. It all depended on how the King felt at the time. The executioner slowly lowered the prisoner to their boiling fate directly below them. After a few moments of excruciating agony, the executioner would pull on the chains to raise the prisoner. The crowds of gathered spectators would see the flesh slowly boiling on the prisoner's reddened body before the executioner once again lowered them to their fate. This process was repeated multiple times to prolong the torture. Records show that people were boiled for up to 2 hours before dying.

Whilst this wasn't a new form of torture, it was enforced in law during the reign of King Henry VIII.

The most famous of prisoners to be boiled alive was a man called Richard Roose. On 18th February 1531, Richard Roose, a cook, genuinely thought it would be funny to put a laxative in the pottage of John Fisher, the Bishop of Rochester. So, he added bad yeast to the pottage mix. It wasn't only the Bishop who was eating at the time. He had sixteen guests. Once the food had been eaten, the leftovers were also provided to the poor, who were gathered outside. Every person who ate the pottage fell ill, extremely ill. Two people died from eating it. The Bishop himself had chosen not to eat, so he was spared being poisoned. Roose was arrested and admitted what he had done, claiming he had meant no harm and that it was only a joke.

When the King became aware of this, he was horrified and wanted to devise a particularly gruesome death for Roose. He immediately passed the Act of Poisoning (1531), providing the right to boil a person alive as an appropriate sentence for treason. The Act specifically named Roose. And so it was, on 15th April 1532, Richard Roose was boiled alive until dead, in public at Smithfield. According to records, some women fainted at the sight and sound of Roose's agony as he slowly boiled to death.

Red-Hot Poker

Red-hot pokers were used during mediaeval and Tudor times to brand prisoners and visibly disfigure them. Some torturers liked to use a heated poker to melt the eyeballs of prisoners during interrogation.

Perhaps King Edward II was the most well-known of the victims of the red-hot poker. He was the King of England from 1307 until 1327. He killed and exiled many knights and powerful land barons. His wife was sent to France to negotiate a peace treaty. Instead, she refused to return and sided with the powerful land baron Roger Mortimer, who had previously been exiled by the King. Mortimer returned with a small army, invaded England, and Edward II fled to Wales, where he was eventually captured. He was imprisoned in Berkeley Castle and forced to abdicate in favour of his son (King Edward III).

The story didn't just end there. Mortimer became paranoid about the many plots to rescue Edward II, so it was eventually decided to end these rescue attempts by killing the deposed King. Mortimer hatched a plot to bring about the King's demise in the most painful and humiliating way that would leave no visible marks on the King's body.

On the night of 21st September 1327, the killers held down the imprisoned King and shoved a red-hot poker up his bottom. This burnt his bowels and internal organs. It is said that his screams could be heard far beyond the walls of the castle.

Oubliette

Many prisoners were thrown into the oubliette and never came out. The word oubliette comes from the French term 'oublier', which means 'to forget'.

The oubliette would most often be located at the bottom of a dungeon. It was a pit or a narrow vertical hole just large enough for an individual to stand up. There would be no room for them to lie down, crouch or sit. The prisoner would either be thrown into the pit or lowered into the narrow shaft. The rope would then quickly be pulled up, and the trapdoor above would be slammed shut. The prisoner would be trapped there with nothing more than their thoughts and perhaps sometimes a hungry, inquisitive rat for company. They would then be forgotten. This was, after all, the very purpose of an oubliette ... somewhere to place a prisoner where they can be forgotten about altogether.

Escape from an oubliette was almost impossible. The only entrance and exit points were from the ceiling far above the prisoner. Even if they were somehow able to climb up the walls, there was still a trapdoor to negotiate. For those prisoners thrown into the oubliette, perhaps to soften up before an interrogation, food and water might occasionally be thrown down for them.

Those prisoners who were truly forgotten about and left to die would suffer a prolonged and painful death, lasting between three weeks and two months. Once dead, the bodies would not be recovered. They would be left to be eaten by rats.

One oubliette with a gruesome reputation can be found in Leap Castle in Coolderry, Ireland. This had spikes embedded into the floor to increase the pain and suffering of the prisoners.

Sometimes, the oubliette would be built directly below the toilets, so raw sewage would cover the prisoner, swiftly bringing about disease. This is the case with the oubliette in Warwick Castle.

Intestinal Crank

The intestinal crank was often used to extract information from prisoners. It was classed as capital punishment because it was pointless to stop once it started. The prisoner would always die, either through pain, the massive trauma of organ failure or excessive blood loss.

Here's the technical part ... The prisoner would be laid flat and tied to a table. Next, a hole would be made in their abdomen. The upper part of the intestine would then be attached to the crank with a hook. When the crank was rotated, it would slowly extract the intestines from the prisoner's abdomen. You can only imagine the prisoner's screams and the slopping noises as their intestines slowly wrap their way around the crank, inch by inch. This was a prolonged process as the intestine measures between 3-6 metres (9-18 feet) in length.

Even when the prisoners fell unconscious during the procedure, a good torturer always had methods to bring them back to consciousness once more, so they could extract more information whilst they endured further suffering until they died.

Immurement

Immurement was a method of capital punishment where the victim would be buried alive.

There were two types of immurement. In the first, the victim would be sealed into their tomb and left to suffocate to death. Sometimes they can be placed into a coffin or bricked up behind a wall. The other type would see the victim sealed behind the wall which had been drilled with small air holes, enabling them to breathe. After days of writhing in agony, they would eventually die of starvation and dehydration. Many would end their days so delirious with starvation they would try to eat part of their own body just to stay alive.

When Thornton Abbey in Lincolnshire was excavated in 1722, amongst the ruins, they found the skeleton of a person who had been immured behind a wall. In that small enclosure, they also found a table at which the skeleton was seated, a candlestick and a book. Some historians believe this to be the remains of Thomas de Gretham, the fourteenth Abbott suspected to be a heretic who practised the dark arts.

Roasting

We've already read about burning being used as a punishment for commoners. Roasting is a variation of this punishment where the offender was hanged in chains over a large fire and left to roast in excruciating pain slowly.

Records show that Sir. John Oldcastle was convicted of heresy and imprisoned in the Tower of London. He later escaped and led a rebellion against the King. He was captured and formally sentenced to death on 14th December 1417. Records show that he was roasted on the gallows at St. Giles's Fields, London.

The Bodies of The Executed

In 1540, King Henry VIII passed a law which granted the Company of Barber-Surgeons an entitlement to the bodies of four executed criminals each year. It was recognised that barbers and surgeons were required to perform dissections and practice their trade. This was the only legal supply of corpses available at the time, just four bodies a year.

During the reign of King George II, the Murder Act was passed in 1751. The Act recognised that execution alone was still too good for the fate of a murderer. Consequently, some other mark must be placed on the convicted person's body. It required that *"in no case whatsoever shall the body of any murderer be ... buried."* This released many more bodies for dissection and experimentation by surgeons as it became lawful to provide the bodies of executed people for dissection.

Gibbets!

Gibbeting was introduced into law in 1751, empowering judges to gibbet the bodies of those executed for murder. Those executed were either to be publicly dissected or left *"hanging in chains."*

The gibbets were the structures from which the bodies of the executed were hanged in chains. There were gibbets on most main roads into London and other towns and cities.

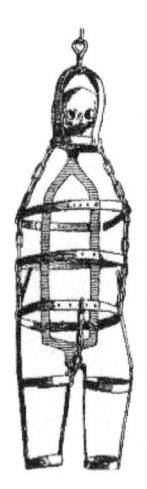

The bodies would often be left until the clothes had completely rotted away and sometimes until the flesh had entirely decomposed. The bodies were hung from chains, arranged on spikes, or hung in body-shaped iron cages. For those who had been executed by being hanged, drawn and quartered, the four body parts would be separated and gibbeted at different locations.

For those living near a gibbet, it was a very unpleasant experience. After the crowds of spectators disappeared, they would be left with the stench of rotting corpses for months and sometimes years. The smell would sometimes be so overpowering the residents had to close their windows. The metal cages and chains on the gibbets were not properly oiled. They would often creak in the wind, further distressing nearby residents.

Whilst there is no doubt that gibbeting was a gruesome sight, it failed to act as a deterrent and crime rates did not fall. Gibbeting finally came to an end in 1832.

Squashed Into Submission

For centuries, if an accused person refused to plead either guilty or not guilty, they would literally be squashed into submitting a plea. This often occurred with a wooden board placed over the accused's body. Heavy stones or iron weights were gradually added in increments, pressing the body until they either entered a plea or suffered broken bones, asphyxia and death.

In 1406 Lord Chief Justice Gascoigne sentenced two robbers. They refused to enter any plea, whether guilty or not guilty. From this moment on, this became an acceptable method to extract a plea from the accused. In this case, the robbers appear to have pretended not to be able to talk in an attempt to avoid entering a plea. Their fate was to be chained in iron to the ground and have weights gradually applied to their bodies until they could bear no more. This became a common practice, so much that Newgate Prison had a dedicated Press Yard, the sight of which was enough to strike fear in prisoners.

The final prisoner to be pressed was John Weekes. On 11th August 1735, he stood trial at the Lewes Assizes, accused of robbery and the murder of Elizabeth Symonds. He refused to enter a plea. He was therefore found guilty and sentenced to be squashed until such a time that he entered a plea. This should have taken place in a prison cell but instead was carried out in full view on the gaol grounds. He was forced to the ground, and a board was placed over him. Some reports state the board used was a prison door. Onto this board were placed weights in 100lb increments. After 300lbs had been added, Weekes appeared to be close to death, so an additional 50lbs was added. Weekes still refused to enter a plea, at which point, the executioner running out of weight, decided to lay on top of the board. Weighing 16-17 stones, this killed Weekes instantly.

Finally, any form of squashing a prisoner into submission was abolished in 1827.

Chapter Eight

Food & Drink

They say you can go for three days without water and three weeks without food.

Food and drink play such an essential part in our lives. We have them multiple times a day, and like fire, shelter and water, we need them to survive.

Throughout my time researching for this book, I have noticed the pre-occupation of the British lawmakers with passing laws about our food and drink. Due to the level of importance that we have attached to food, in centuries gone by, some of the penalties for breaking the food and drink-related laws have been very severe. You were considered a total menace to society and moved from town to town.

Thankfully, sanity has prevailed, and we may now partake in a hearty Christmas Day feast on a table adorned with fanciful decorations and a full plate of mince pies.

Illegal to Eat More Than 2 Courses During Meal Times

In 1309 King Edward II passed a law against the *'outrageous and excessive multitude of meats and dishes which the great men of the Kingdom had used, and still used, in their castles.'* In 1336, King Edward III attempted to pass a new law to address *'the excessive and overmany sorts of costly meats which the People of this Realm have used.'*

Bizarrely, it enacted that no man should eat or cause to be served more than two courses per meal, except during Christmas, when three courses may be served. To cheat the system, people were trying to have soup as an extra course and claiming it was a 'sauce' to accompany their food, like ketchup or horseradish. This law contained a clause to prevent this.

Common punishments for breaking the sumptuary laws were the confiscation of the item itself and a fine.

It remained law for 520 years until it was repealed in 1856.

Illegal to Eat Mince Pies on Christmas Day

This is a tricky one. There was a law of sorts that would have prohibited the eating of mince pies on Christmas Day. Although it appears this was only a prohibited activity on Christmas Day in 1644. The reality was that this was a mandated day of fasting. The Cambridge Dictionary definition for 'fasting' is 'to eat no food for a period of time'. So, it wasn't just mince pies but all sorts of food that were forbidden on that date.

In an attempt to put a stop to these excesses of food and poor behaviour from the English, primarily-Christian population, on 24th August 1642, the Puritans passed a law called 'An Ordinance for the better observation of the monthly Fast.'

This ordinance required that the last Wednesday of each month was a day of fasting to remember Christ and to repent for our sins. This didn't become an issue until two years later when Christmas Day in 1644 fell on the last Wednesday of the month. Surely, they didn't expect people not to celebrate Christmas Day? Well, yes, they certainly did, and after requests were made to waive the fast on that Christmas Day of 1644, Parliament's response on 19th December 1644 was ... to issue another law (Ordinance to observe the Monthly Fast, especially on the day which heretofore was called The Feast of the Nativity of Our Saviour).

And so, Christmas Day in 1644 was legally a mandatory day of fasting. Mince pies weren't banned but they were frowned upon as the day was set aside for fasting.

You Can Be Fined for Interfering with a Cup of Tea

As tea is such an important drink to the British, I feel it's only fair to give a little history lesson here. Legend tells us that tea was first discovered in 2737 BC by Chinese Emperor Shennong, who saw that some leaves from a nearby tree blew into his recently boiled drinking water. He noticed the leaves changed the colour and taste of the water and seemed to have some therapeutic properties.

The first record of tea sold in England was in a coffee house in London in 1657. We know from the diary of Samuel Pepys that on Tuesday 25th September 1660, he tasted his first cup of tea which he referred to as 'a China drink'.

Whenever anything new enters common circulation, there will always be someone trying to profit or deceive people from it. In this case, some very naughty people have taken it upon themselves over the centuries to knowingly pass off some other substance as a pleasant cup of tea. This practice is known as adulteration.

Generally, tea is adulterated through means of some additives to the tea, especially colouring. It was sold by weight, so unscrupulous local vendors often introduced impurities by adding iron filings, clay and gypsum to add extra weight to the tea they were selling.

King George I passed the earliest law to counter this crime to our tea drinkers, in 1724. This was aimed at those who mixed tea with other substances. The penalty was forfeiture of the offending 'tea' and a fine. This early law only dealt with those who manufactured the impure tea, not those who sold it.

His successor, King George II passed a law in 1730 which specifically noted that additives were being used deceitfully to dye tea leaves previously used. It also focused on the dealers who sold the tea, which was missed in the earlier 1724 law. The penalty was a £10 fine for each pound in weight of adulterated or imitation tea.

Tea wasn't the only item that was adulterated. Coffee was also considered fair game until a law was passed covering it in 1718. This provided a penalty of a £20 fine. This was eventually repealed in 1958.

A Baker's Dozen

In 1266, King Henry III passed a law that regulated the price of a loaf of bread and a quantity of ale in relation to the current price of wheat. This was our first law to regulate the production and sale of food.

The usual punishment for those caught cheating their customers was a heavy fine for the first few times. If the baker didn't change their deceitful ways, repeat offences would be punished with a visit to the pillory or to gaol, followed by their being banned from being a baker altogether.

The public pillory was a very humiliating punishment. It was known as the 'stretch neck'. The offender's head would be locked into position, and their hands would be locked into holes on either side to prevent them from moving. Often their head would also be shaven. Passing members of the public would see the deceitful baker in the village pillory and be able to throw rotten food or other offensive items at the baker.

The penalties for deceitful bakers in the City of London were far more severe. The offending bakers would have been dragged around crowded streets on a hurdle for the first offence. For the second offence, they were dragged through the streets on a hurdle to the pillory, where they would be locked in it for an hour. For a third offence, the baker would then be dragged through the streets on a hurdle, his baker's oven would be broken up, and he would be forced to give up baking forever.

The constant anxiety caused by possible accusations of wrongdoing and the fear of being punished, caused many bakers to throw in extra bread when sold. This is where the term 'a Baker's Dozen' is believed to have originated. For example, if a dozen loaves were ordered, the baker would throw in extra bread to ensure that any inadvertent shortfall in weight was made up.

A record from 1360 shows that a baker in Suffolk named John Baker (very appropriate!) was fined 24 pence and placed in the pillory for breaking this law.

The bread law was finally repealed in 1863.

Supermarket Sweep

Over the last few months, I have noticed several customers in my local supermarket opening packets of food and chomping on the contents whilst walking around. This seems to be a perfectly innocent occurrence that I often see taking place. Quite often, a parent will give the contents of a multi-pack to placate their screaming toddler in the trolley. The usual practice is to place the empty wrapper or pack on the checkout conveyor belt and pay for it on the way out, along with the rest of their shopping.

This is technically a criminal offence of theft.

This even seems at odds with how police are trained. They are taught that shoplifters can be arrested once they pass *"the final point of payment."* Although, I suspect this is more to do with ensuring sufficient evidence and criminal intent to make out the full theft offence. When you purchase your shopping and pay for it at the tills, it is only at this point that the ownership of that property legally transfers to you. Before that time, if you do anything that deprives the current owner of the right to their property, you have treated it as your own and committed the offence of theft.

Whilst slipping a few grapes into your mouth and walking around the supermarket may seem like a minor indiscretion in the grand scheme of things, it's important to remember how destructive having a criminal record for theft can be. A dishonesty offence can have serious repercussions, which could severely affect a person's life.

Chapter Nine
FOREIGNERS

No-one wants to feel like an outcast or a foreigner in another country. Sadly, many laws have been passed throughout our great history encouraging hatred towards those not from this sceptred isle.

Like most laws, they were passed at a time when it was considered to be in the best interests of the common people. Despite the many myths that over time have been weaved into our history surrounding the love-hate relationship we have with foreigners, it has, on occasion, led to people taking up arms against the Welsh, Scottish and Irish, and vice versa.

You would imagine the death penalty was reserved for those who committed terrible atrocities against humankind, like murder, torture or robbery. As you will see in this chapter, the death penalty was given in some cases just for being foreign.

Despite all this doom and gloom, there have more recently been some humorous examples surrounding the laws related to 'foreigners.'

Death Penalty if You Were Seen in the Company of Gypsies

In 1505 we saw the first officially recorded Gypsies in England. They were thought to have come from Egypt and hence became known as 'Egyptians'. The term later became corrupted to 'Gypsies'. However, some parish records show that Irish Travellers occupied England before this time. Immediately, they were seen as a public nuisance with accusations that Gypsies were constantly deceiving people, claiming to tell fortunes, committing robberies and other heinous acts.

So, in 1530, King Henry VIII passed a law, preventing any Gypsies from lawfully entering England. It also required all remaining Gypsies to leave England within 16 days. If they failed to leave, they were immediately deported. Any property that gypsies had stolen was to be restored to its rightful owner.

Not only was it now illegal to be a Gypsy in England, but in 1554, Queen Mary changed the law providing the punishment of death if you were found to be a Gypsy. Under the law, Gypsies were permitted to leave England and not return. Failure to do so within one month meant instant death. It also made it an offence, punishable by the same death penalty, if you were just found in the company of 'Egyptians' (Gypsies).

It wasn't until 100 years later, in the 1650s, that we see the last recorded case of a Gypsy hanged in Suffolk. At the time, other Gypsies were transported to the Americas. In 1783, during the reign of King George III, another law was passed, which made it an offence to even 'pretend' to be a Gypsy. These laws were finally repealed in 1856.

Welsh People Banned From Owning Land in Wales

Since the death of the last native Prince of Wales, Llywelyn ap Gruffydd, in 1282, the Welsh had to endure several harsh laws after its conquest by King Edward I of England. They were forbidden from living in borough towns, such as Conwy and Caernarfon. They weren't allowed the same trading rights as the English ... but things were about to get considerably worse for them.

Owain Glyndŵr, a Lord from the Welsh Marches (the areas of England that border Wales), was initially loyal to the English Crown and fought alongside the English army against the Scottish in the 1380s. In 1400, he had a land dispute with Baron Grey of Ruthyn, who had seized control of some of his land. Glyndŵr appealed to Parliament and the courts, but he was ignored. This land dispute spiralled out of control, and from that moment on, the Welsh rallied behind Glyndŵr in a Welsh uprising. On 16th September 1400, Glyndŵr was proclaimed

Prince of Wales. This rebellion against English rule lasted for a further 15 years.

In 1402, the English Parliament under King Henry IV passed a law which banned Welshmen from owning a castle, except those from the time of King Edward I.

The problem is that these laws encouraged more Welsh people to join the rebellion. The Welsh retook much of their land and castles. When news of their gains against the English reached the Scottish and the French, they sent additional military support to bolster the Welsh uprising.

Despite this military assistance, the English had far superior numbers and greater resources. By 1409, the English had recaptured much of Wales, forcing Glyndŵr to take refuge in the sieged Harlech Castle. Glyndŵr, however, had other plans and escaped into the night, disguised as an old man. These Penal Laws were finally repealed in 1624 by King James I.

An Englishman Could Not Be Convicted by a Welshman in Wales

As a result of the Glyndŵr Rising and the land disputes between the English and the Welsh, in 1402, the English Parliament passed the Penal Laws. These were a series of laws that severely restricted the rights of the Welsh. One of the very first laws passed confidently stated,

'Englishman shall not be convict[ed] by Welshman in Wales'.

Welsh People Banned From Speaking Welsh in Wales

This title may appear a little misleading, but it was technically accurate, or at least in schools and courts. Cymraeg, or Welsh as the language is known in English, has taken a battering over the centuries.

During the reign of King Henry VIII, The Laws in Wales Acts were passed in 1535 and 1542. These laws annexed Wales to the Kingdom of England, making English law enforceable in Wales and banning the use of the Welsh language in court proceedings. At the time, over 90% of the people in Wales spoke Welsh. Those who didn't speak English had issues getting work and even found that the Welsh language was suppressed in schools.

Children would be routinely punished in schools in Wales if they were heard speaking in Welsh. There are reported cases as far back as 1798 where Welsh-speaking children would be singled out and forced to wear a piece of wood attached to a rope around their necks. Upon the piece of wood was inscribed the letters 'W.N.' This stood for 'Welsh Not'. The last school child wearing the Welsh Not would be punished at the end of each day. This could be in the form of receiving lashings or a caning from the headmaster. Evidence indicates that the W.N. was still used in Wales as recently as the 1940s.

This was the same in the workplace. There are reports that during the 18th and 19th centuries, miners who spoke Welsh could lose their jobs.

In the 1960s, the Welsh Language Society began a campaign to deface or remove English-only road signs in Wales. Many of the English road signs were painted over with green paint. This eventually led to bilingual signs along the main Welsh roads.

In 2016, a new law came into force in Wales which required that all signs be in Welsh first, followed by the English translation. This widespread change to bilingual road signs did, at times, have some rather amusing outcomes. For example, in 2006, a bilingual pedestrian sign on the streets of Cardiff instructed pedestrians in Welsh to *"edrychwch i'r chwith"* (look left). However, the English translation stated, *"look right"*. In another case, a sign placed at the entrance to a Swansea supermarket read in Welsh, *"Nid wyf yn y swyddfa ar hyn o bryd. Anfonwch unrhyw waith i'w gyfieithu".* The English translation being, *"I am not in the office at the moment. Send any work to be translated."* Someone had not switched off their Out of Office email reply.

King Henry VIII's Laws in Wales Acts were finally repealed between 1993 and 1995.

Illegal to Be Welsh in Chester During the Hours of Darkness

A common myth states that you are entirely within your rights to shoot a Welsh person with a longbow if found after midnight in Chester. There are other variants that state they have to be found within the city walls of Chester. There is no knowing from where this myth originated. Still, it is likely to have come from a Chester City law passed on 4th September 1403 as a response to the Glyndŵr Rising. During this time, Chester was under frequent attack by the Welsh.

After the Glyndŵr Rising, the Earl of Chester (shortly to become King Henry V) sought to impose a curfew on the Welsh to reduce the likelihood of future attacks. He ordered that *"all Welsh people and Welsh sympathisers should be expelled from the city; none should enter the city before sunrise or stay after sunset on pain of decapitation."* There's no mention of longbows or crossbows, just that the Welsh people would be beheaded.

There is no indication that this law was ever repealed. Still, thankfully, modern-day laws provide a suitable deterrence to prevent the cold-blooded murder of Welsh people within the city walls of Chester.

Shooting Welsh in Hereford

Unfortunately, if you were Welsh in mediaeval and Tudor times, your outlook would be bleak if you tried to cross the border into Hereford. As with Welsh men being found in Chester, a myth also exists surrounding a 'right' in law to shoot a Welsh man in Cathedral Close, Hereford, at any time of the day, provided it is with a longbow.

Again, as with the Welsh found in Chester, it is most likely to have come from a local law due to the Glyndŵr Rising. This comes with the same warning: any attempt to murder a Welsh man by shooting them with a longbow would these days be classed as murder.

It Is Perfectly Legal in York to Shoot a Scotsman with a Crossbow, Except on Sundays

I can tell you that, as with any alleged freedom to shoot Welsh men in Chester or Hereford, the shooting of Scottish folk in York is also illegal. The myth alleges that it is legal in York to shoot a Scotsman with a crossbow, except on Sundays. Unless that is, they are either found in a state of drunkenness or with a weapon and then it's perfectly acceptable to shoot them, even on a Sunday, although still not with a crossbow. The Law Commission clarified the legal position by stating, "*It is illegal to shoot a Welsh or Scottish (or any other) person regardless of the day, location or choice of weaponry.*"

Was Berwick-upon-Tweed at War With Russia From 1854 to 1966?

Berwick-upon-Tweed in Northumberland is the northernmost town in England, just 2.5 miles south of the Scottish border. In 1502, King Henry VII of England and King James IV of Scotland signed the Treaty of Perpetual Peace. This Treaty ended centuries of conflict between the English and Scottish in the town. Even then, it remained quasi-independent and afforded the status *"of but not within the Kingdom of England."*

With the passing of the Wales and Berwick-upon-Tweed Act (1746), any future laws automatically included both of these regions. However, Berwick-upon-Tweed continued as a quasi-independent region long after the passing of this law. This created somewhat of a problem when Britain entered the Crimean War in 1854 after Russia decided to invade the Crimea. Britain had no option but to protect its interests and declare war on Russia in March 1854. It was believed that when Queen Victoria signed the declaration of war, she did so on behalf of *"Great Britain, Ireland, Berwick-upon-Tweed and all British Dominions."*

The war ended in 1856, when the major powers met in Paris to sign the Treaty of Paris. This required Russia to return all occupied Ottoman territory. It is alleged that *Berwick-upon-Tweed* was accidentally left out from the wording of the Treaty. This diplomatic mistake was discovered in the spring of

1914. For years, it was therefore believed that the town of Berwick-upon-Tweed was still at war with Russia.

In 1965, the Foreign Office confirmed that they had reviewed the matter thirty years previously but had found no evidence to suggest this was the case. So, it was deemed that no remaining conflict existed between Berwick-upon-Tweed and Russia. To further cement this, in 1966, an official visited Berwick from Soviet Russia and allegedly signed an unofficial 'peace treaty' with the then Mayor of Berwick, Robert Knox, to formally mark the cessation of any hostility.

Chapter Ten
FUN & GAMES

Over the years, we have been limited as to which games and forms of entertainment we could actually partake in from one time to another.

Football wasn't allowed. Cricket was banned for centuries. Even Tiddlywinks was forbidden. As recently as the late twentieth century, daytime television programmes were illegal, and no-one was permitted to attend the theatre or cinema on Sundays.

In this chapter, we delve into why the past governments sought to make our ancestors so miserable, banning almost every popular form of entertainment but allowing some of the more hazardous pastimes.

The Unlawful Games

As one of our greatest military achievements, archery became the central focus of various laws over the years, requiring its continual practice to ensure Britain maintained a strong defensive capability. In 1388, King Richard II passed a law requiring archery to be practised by all labourers, servants, artificers, and victuallers (those licensed to sell alcohol). This also imposed a ban on several games, including one with rules similar to cricket. This was repeated in a law passed by King Henry IV in 1409 with a punishment of six days' imprisonment for those who refused to obey.

Archery wasn't the only popular sport. For centuries, we continued to enjoy our quiet village pastimes without restriction. Sadly, this all changed in the mid-sixteenth century when King Henry VIII feared that people were quickly losing their proficiency in archery and instead preferring what he called senseless *"diverse and many unlawful games."* As a result, in 1541, he passed a law called '*The Unlawful Games Act*'.

This law required all men to practice their bow and arrow skills regularly. Nearly all men under the age of 60 were required to keep bows and arrows for shooting. It also required those aged 17 and above to "*keep a bow and 4 arrows*" and boys aged between 7 and 16 to "*have a bow and 2 shafts.*" The penalty for not obeying this law was a fine of 6 shillings and 8 pence.

This law remained in force, in full, on the statute books until much of it was repealed during Victorian times in 1845. It was finally only fully repealed in 1960.

Cockfighting in Schools

'Cocking' as it used to be known, was once considered a perfectly respectable pastime in schools and wider society. The Romans originally introduced the sport and gradually, since mediaeval times, it became very popular in Britain. Cock pits were a common sight in most villages, and spectators regularly travelled from afar to attend a cockfight. A twelfth-century account of the City of London written by William Fitzstephen shows that it was customary for boys to take gamecocks to school to fight on Shrove Tuesdays. He noted how their classrooms would be transformed into cock pits.

In 1607, the earliest known book on the sport of cockfighting was written by George Wilson. This book entitled 'The Commendation of Cocks and Cock Fighting' became the rulebook for cockfighting in schools.

Occasionally, small silver bells were presented as prizes during school cockfights. Records also show that teachers received payments from the schoolboys for bringing in their cockerels. Spectators were also permitted to attend the school to watch the cockfights upon payment.

Cockfighting remained a common pastime until the late eighteenth century, with small pockets of activity still occurring into the early nineteenth century. By that time, people were becoming more concerned with animal welfare. The sport gradually became less popular after an animal welfare law was passed in 1835. It wasn't until 1849 that cockfighting was banned in England and Wales. In 1895, cockfighting was eventually banned in Scotland.

Illegal to Play Cricket

Quite how cricket became a national game, or even the origins of the game itself, are unknown. Records from the early 1300s show Prince Edward, the son of King Edward I, playing a game known as '*creag*'.

Perhaps one of the key reasons cricket was not documented during its earlier years is that many of the records from that time originated from the church. Evidence shows that from the 14th century onwards, the church started to feel that playing sports and games was leading to bad behaviour. This was especially apparent with many sports being played on Sunday, the Sabbath. Around the same time, we begin to see a rise in the number of laws banning various sports and games. In 1366, King Edward III encouraged the practice of archery and sought to discourage the playing of certain other games which would interfere with archery practice. This would undoubtedly have seen cricket frowned upon as one of the sports denounced as being dishonourable.

In 1477, King Edward IV passed a law which added "*closh, kailes, half-bowl, hand-in, hand-out, and queckboard*" to the list of banned sports and games because they interfered with the practice of archery. '*Hand-in, hand-out*' was the sport of cricket in its early years. The penalty for playing a game of cricket was two years imprisonment and a £10 fine. Anyone found allowing a game of cricket to be played on his premises would suffer three years imprisonment and a £20 fine. In addition, all the cricket equipment would be burned.

In 1728, King George II passed a law banning Unlawful Games, including cricket. Over the centuries, it appears that many played cricket illegally. It wasn't until 1748 that cricket was declared a legal sport.

Cricket could very well have been outlawed just a few years later, after it led to the death of a very famous person. Frederick Louis, the Prince of Wales, was widely known to have enjoyed playing cricket. Sadly, he died during a cricket match on 31st March 1751. At the time, it was believed a cricket ball had hit him in the chest, causing a burst abscess in his lungs.

Illegal to Play Football

By mediaeval standards, modern-day football would seem like a kindergarten five-a-side match. The 'football' used was an inflated pig's bladder. Very few rules existed. It was a brutal, violent game often played between neighbouring villages, sometimes resulting in death.

In 1314, whilst King Edward II was fighting the war in Scotland with Robert the Bruce, he banned football from being played in the City of London. Several London merchants had complained that playing football in the streets was disturbing the peace. On 13th April that year, the first ban on football was enforced which provided the penalty of imprisonment, although this only applied in London.

In 1349, his son, King Edward III, decided to ban football nationally. This was more for reasons of ensuring national security. He was concerned that playing football distracted men from practising archery. Archers were England's valuable defence on the battlefield. With so many families wiped out during the bubonic plague (Black Death) between 1346-1353, it was necessary to ensure enough men of fighting age were proficient in archery skills.

In 1388, King Richard II decreed that servants and labourers should cease playing football and use bows and arrows instead. Again, the motivation behind this was to enhance England's defensive capability. In 1409, King Henry IV re-affirmed this law and added a punishment of six days imprisonment for those who broke the law.

In 1477, King Edward IV further banned football and many other sports and games. He required all able-bodied people to practice with a bow and arrow.

We know that King Henry VIII was a keen sportsman in his earlier years. Records from 1526 also show that the King had one pair of leather football boots in his collection. In 1541, he passed a law called The Unlawful Games Act, which effectively banned football.

Throughout the Elizabethan period, there seems to have been a relaxation of the ban on sports. However, there were still occasional outbursts of violence associated with the game. In one such occurrence in 1608, the authorities in Manchester became irritated with the damage it was causing, with balls breaking windows and leading to general disorder in the town. As a result, that year, football was banned in Manchester.

Football suffered a brief respite in 1618 when King James I issued the '*Declaration of Sports*' (also known as the Book of Sports). He instructed Christians to play football every Sunday afternoon following worship. However, in 1625, The Sunday Observance Act was passed which once again banned playing football on Sundays. During the Civil War, those caught playing football were fined or placed in the village stocks. Following the Restoration of the monarchy in 1660, football started to rise again in popularity.

With the incredible recent successes of the England women's national football team (the Lionesses), it's hard to imagine that in 1921, women were banned from playing at both English and Scottish football league grounds. This ban was only lifted as recently as the 1970s.

Illegal to Sing Happy Birthday in Public

One of the most well-known songs in the world, sung by billions of people each year, is *"Happy Birthday..."* it's the staple of birthday parties worldwide. According to the Guinness World Records in 1998, it is the most recognised song in the English language, followed by *"For He's a Jolly Good Fellow."* However, something may have slipped your notice over the last few years. You will find very few television shows, cinema movies or public performances in which the song 'Happy Birthday' is sung. This is because, despite being sung by billions around the world, everyone in the film industry was aware that this song was copyrighted. Each time it was used, it had to be properly licenced, with a hefty fee paid to the licensing company. In fact, for years, restaurant staff found ways to get around this by singing other versions of birthday songs so they wouldn't have to pay a licence fee for the public performance of this copyrighted song. Most people were unaware the song is copyrighted, hence why it was often sung at private birthday parties because this was not classed as a 'public performance'.

The iconic melody to the Happy Birthday song was created around 1893 by the sisters Patty and Mildred Hill from Kentucky as a children's song. They originally called the melody *'Good Morning to You'*. It is unknown whether the Hill sisters also wrote the lyrics to 'Happy Birthday'.

The whole matter was brought before the U.S. courts in 2015 when a group of artists challenged the copyright licence held by music publishing company Warner/Chappell Music. For decades, Warner/Chappell has collected an estimated $2 million annually from people who wanted to licence the 'Happy Birthday' song. Warner/Chappell argued in court that they were the rightful copyright owners.

It was challenged in court by a group of artists who claimed to have found proof that the 'Happy Birthday' song was actually in the public domain and available for anyone to use for any purpose freely.

Illegal to Borrow Library Books if You Have Food Poisoning, Diarrhoea or Rabies

Towards the end of the Victorian period, the public had heightened anxiety about the spread of disease. This was due to people living much closer together and poor hygiene standards. Nevertheless, there became what was known as the 'great book scare' when members of the public feared that they could catch an infectious disease from library books. A law was passed in 1875 to deal with public hygiene. Whilst it didn't specifically refer to library books, it nevertheless banned the lending of any "*bedding clothing rags or other things*" that had been exposed to infection.

In 1907, the law began to address the spread of disease through the lending of library books. From that point on, anyone with an infectious disease was forbidden to borrow or return a library book. It stated, "*If any person knows that he is suffering from an infectious disease he shall not take any book or use or cause any book to be taken for his use from any public or circulating library.*" The punishment for this offence was a fine of up to 40 shillings.

The law was updated in 1984. It made it illegal for anyone suffering from a notifiable disease to borrow a book from a public library. Once you had borrowed a library book, it was then illegal to provide it to anyone suffering from a notifiable disease. If you borrowed a book and subsequently caught a notifiable disease whilst the book was still in your possession, you had first to notify the local authority that you had been exposed to infection before returning the book to the public library. Interestingly, the term '*notifiable disease*' covered many different types of disease, including leprosy, cholera, measles, the plague (Black Death!), rabies, infectious bloody diarrhoea and even food poisoning.

Illegal to Have a Party

In the 1980s, the rave scene crossed the Atlantic from the USA and captured many young partygoers' imaginations. By the early 1990s, raves had become commonplace and considered by many as anti-social and a public nuisance. The government felt they had to address this and passed a law in 1990 which allowed authorities to fine the organisers of illegal raves and parties up to £20,000. This was a lot of money for a fine and most likely an attempt to shock and deter would-be rave hosts. This didn't deter the hardcore rave organisers, who looked for new ways to outwit the police. They soon discovered a technique to evade discovery by the police, leaving the party location a secret until shortly before the event. This prevented the police from being able to stop and turn away ravers before they arrived at the illegal gatherings. Organisers started broadcasting the details of the parties at the last minute via pirate radio stations. This later turned into ravers being asked to call a telephone number where they could hear a pre-recorded voicemail message advising them of the party location.

This cat and mouse game continued until things reached a head between 22nd and 29th May 1992 when 20,000 people turned up to a week-long illegal rave on the idyllic and otherwise quiet Castlemorton Common in Worcestershire. Locals described the scene as like something from a Mad Max film. What was supposed to be a small music festival quickly spiralled out of control and went down in history as the UK's largest-ever illegal rave. The subsequent court trial cost £4 million and led to the government passing a new law in 1994. This gave the police extensive powers to target party gatherings of more than a hundred people listening to music during the night. It also enabled them to stop vehicles within a 5-mile (8kms) radius of the party and turn them away.

Illegal to Hypnotise The Audience on TV

We have probably come a long way from the days of the Victorian evil hypnotist wearing a top hat and dark cloak, swinging a pocket watch and telling his victim to look into his eyes. The local council must issue a license before hypnosis can be performed on stage. Conducting an unlicensed performance can result in a large fine. This goes back to concerns raised over hypnosis in the 1950s, which resulted in a hypnosis law being passed in 1952. From that moment on, hypnosis performances were licensed, and hypnosis broadcast over television was banned.

The rules were tested to their limit by Channel 4 on 18th September 2009, when they broadcast a programme featuring the illusionist Derren Brown's 'How to Control the Nation'. As part of the programme, Brown played a short film which he claimed would make some television viewers feel stuck to their chairs. Brown did not state this was hypnosis, and he made no claims to be hypnotising the viewers. Over 3 million people viewed the programme. It is alleged that 1 in 4 viewers were affected by this 'subliminal suggestion'. A Channel 4 spokeswoman claimed they had received 50,000 phone calls within three minutes of the broadcast from viewers who stated they were stuck to their chairs. This programme wasn't hypnosis. It was merely what some might believe to have been hypnosis.

The Saturday Football Blackout

In the early 1960s, the then chairman of Burnley Football Club, Bob Lord, convinced fellow Football League chairmen that televising matches on Saturday afternoons would have a negative impact on the attendance of lower league games. He genuinely believed that if a 3pm match between, for example, Manchester United and Liverpool football clubs were televised, many supporters would rather watch that on television than attend a lower division team match at their stadium. Following this, a gentleman's agreement was reached where a football broadcasting blackout was enforced for all clubs playing Premier League, Football League or FA Cup matches on a Saturday afternoon. The blackout lasted between 2:45pm and 5:15pm. This meant that most Saturday 3pm kick-offs could not be televised in the UK. From that moment on, the TV networks could only show Saturday matches with early or late kick-offs. No law has ever been passed on this matter. However, this early gentleman's agreement nevertheless exists even to this day.

Interestingly, live radio broadcasts are still permitted during the blackout. It is only enforced on televised broadcasts.

Daytime Television Used to Be Illegal

You can switch on the television at any time of the day or night and find something to watch. It might not necessarily be good, but there's always something to watch. Compare that to the situation just a few decades ago, when if you switched the TV on at 3am, you would be met with a black screen. In fact, until 1972, daytime television in the UK was illegal! It was previously felt that daytime TV shows would make the British public lazy.

In 1955, broadcasting restrictions meant that the BBC was only permitted to broadcast a maximum of 5 hours per day. That same year, the commercial channel ITV launched, and both channels were permitted to broadcast up to 7 hours per day. This gradually increased and by 1972, broadcasting restrictions meant that TV channels were only allowed to broadcast 50 hours a week and a maximum of 8 hours in any one day.

Bizarrely, until 1957, there was a ban on television programmes being broadcast between 6pm and 7pm. In what was nicknamed the *'Toddler's Truce'*, it was felt this was the optimal time for parents to put their children to bed. From 7pm onwards, this became prime-time TV. In 1958, this toddler's truce restriction was lifted but not quite how the public might have liked. It was decided that only religious programmes could be aired during that hour.

The broadcasting restrictions were eased for large-scale sporting and State events and other occasions where families would be together, like Christmas Eve, Christmas Day, Boxing Day, New Year's Eve and New Year's Day.

This all changed on 19th January 1972, when all previous broadcasting restrictions were lifted. This wasn't an instant move to fill daytime TV scheduling with content. It occurred very gradually over several years. When the government lifted this restriction, most programmes shown on TV in the mornings were primarily schools-based. ITV also began providing afternoon TV with programmes for the younger viewing audience being shown during the mornings of school holidays. By November 1972, ITV had launched a full daytime schedule which began at 9.30am each day. That same year, the BBC launched its flagship daytime television show called Pebble Mill at One. It was a live television show filled with celebrity interviews and music.

Finally, at 6.30am on 17th January 1983, the BBC launched its first ever breakfast television show on BBC1, Breakfast Time. A couple of weeks later, on 1st February, ITV also launched its first breakfast TV slot, TV-am.

Chapter Eleven

INDECENCY

'*No kissing please, we're British.*' This perfectly sums up the delicate nature of British folk. Outwardly, we may appear stand-offish, uptight and stiff-upper-lipped. History tells us this is most certainly not the case, with many laws passed to protect us from ourselves.

One final word before you delve into this chapter ... Spanko!

The Topless Act

It has become a widely-shared myth that King James I allegedly passed a law called the 'Topless Act', which required young women to be topless when in public. As you probably gathered, I can confirm this is a myth. No such law was passed by King James I. Society was going through a particularly turbulent period. It is possible that the myth referred to King James I of Scotland (1406-1437). He might have been able to get away with such a law in thirteenth-century Scotland when women had even fewer rights.

With all this conversation about topless women, what about men ... or indeed anyone, is it legal to walk around with tops off? In Britain, when the sun comes out during the late spring period, you can often see young gents in public with their tops off. Is this public nudity legal? In fact, do you have to stop at your top, or is it theoretically acceptable to remove more items of clothing? There is no offence of public nudity. However, walking around exposing your intimate parts to passing members of the public will undoubtedly breach various other laws, including indecent exposure and the offence of outraging public decency.

In Scotland, things are slightly different. Under Scots law, any form of indecent behaviour in a public place could constitute an offence of public indecency. In 2006, Stephen Gough, aka 'The Naked Rambler', was arrested at Edinburgh airport after emerging from the aeroplane toilet mid-flight, having removed his clothing on the early morning flight from Southampton to Edinburgh and then refusing to get dressed.

In the privacy of your own garden, you can strip off to your heart's content, sunbathe, perform yoga or do the Gangnam Style dance. Provided your intention is not to cause any alarm or distress to anyone else, it doesn't matter if your neighbours or anyone else can see you. Be warned, however, whilst this is theoretical, and the Crown Prosecution Service has issued guidelines, it wouldn't necessarily stop a visit from the police. A common-sense approach is always preferable.

Shakespeare Banned in Great Yarmouth

When we consider Britain's best-known writers, the names Charles Dickens, Jane Austen, William Shakespeare, Geoffrey Chaucer, Tennyson, and Byron will invariably feature in that list. They are celebrated throughout the nation, with the erection of blue plaques, buildings, roads, and other structures being named after them. However, it would seem one council has taken a particular dislike to the works of William Shakespeare. It is reported that the Great Yarmouth town council previously disapproved of the moral character of some of Shakespeare's works and refused to name any roads after him.

A Freedom of Information request confirmed there are presently no roads within the borough of Great Yarmouth named after Shakespeare's characters.

Whipping Tom & Spring-Heeled Jack

In the early 1970s, a British TV comedy created a character set in Victorian London called '*The Phantom Raspberry Blower of*

Old London Town'. It featured a madman who killed his victims by jumping out of the shadows and frightening them to death by blowing a raspberry at them. As bizarre as this seems, these kind of odd crimes did, in fact, occur on the streets of Victorian London. They were usually crazed opportunists, hoping for a quick grope, but occasionally patterns of behaviour emerged, so often the perpetrators were given nicknames.

One such Victorian fellow was given the nickname '*Whipping Tom*'. This turned out to be two separate crazed attackers in London and Hackney. Both attackers would jump out, surprising women walking alone and smacking them on their bottoms. His escapades started in 1681, in central London, between Fleet Street, Strand and Holborn. He would quietly approach women walking alone in alleyways and courtyards, grab them and bend them over his knee, lifting their dress and spanking them on the bottom, before making his escape. Sometimes, he would accompany his spanks by shouting, "*Spanko!*" On most occasions, he would use his bare hand, but sometimes he used a rod.

He attacked so many women during his short spell of mayhem. His ability to evade the authorities caused a spate of complaints about the ineffectiveness of London's Constabulary. As a result, local vigilante men tried to trap him by dressing up as women to entice Whipping Tom to attack them. Some women even took to carrying small weapons to protect themselves whilst walking late at night. Eventually, a local haberdasher and his accomplice were captured and put on trial.

The second Whipping Tom attacked women in Hackney between 10th October and 1st December 1712. He used a similar method of approaching unaccompanied women walking in the countryside. He would grab and beat them on the bottom with a birch rod. During his reign of terror, he amassed around

70 attacks against frightened local women. Eventually, he was captured and named as Thomas Wallis. He confessed to his offences. He claimed his attacks were an act of revenge on all women after he had been wronged by a woman who had lied about him. A curiously religious man, he said that he planned to attack 100 women before Christmas, then pause during the 12 days of Christmas, resuming his attacks in the New Year.

Another peculiar Victorian character was known as '*Spring-Heeled Jack*'. He enjoyed a 10-year spell in the imaginations of Victorian society. Sightings of him became so common that an official enquiry was set up, following which a suspect was put on trial. At the time, the public believed it was someone wealthy enough to pay for such an elaborate disguise and with enough time on their hands to go around pranking people. It was thought it could even be a mad Marquess.

His story started in October 1837. A young maid called Mary Stevens was walking through Clapham Common when suddenly, a strange figure jumped out at her from a dark alleyway. He repeatedly kissed her on the face and ripped her clothes with what she claimed to have been claws. The following day, a horse and carriage driver crashed his carriage after seeing Spring-Heeled Jack breathing fire and laughing before he leapt over a 9-foot high wall making his escape. The following year, The Times newspaper reported on 19th February that a lady called Jane Alsop answered her front door to a man claiming to be a police officer. He told the lady to bring out a light and said, "*we have caught Spring-Heeled Jack here in the lane.*" Upon taking out a candle to him, she noticed he was wearing a large cloak. She handed him the candle, at which point he ripped off his cloak and vomited blue-and-white flames from his mouth. She described his eyes as appearing like "*red balls of fire.*" He tore her clothes with his long claws, but she managed to escape.

154 BIZARRE LAWS OF THE UK FOR KIDS

Whatever the truth about Spring-Heeled Jack, he was never caught, and no doubt there must have been an original prankster who started it. After just a few weeks, the stories would have become so embellished, not forgetting that Victorians were very superstitious and with some degree of mass hysteria thrown into the mix, Spring-Heeled Jack's legend was born.

Chapter Twelve

JUSTICE

Britain is known worldwide for having a fair, transparent and tolerant justice system. It hasn't always been that way, with all sorts of blood feuds and unfair trials during mediaeval times.

Our justice system has matured over the centuries. We pick up in this chapter from our Anglo-Saxon ancestors with some of their unusual methods for dispensing 'like for like' justice. They say justice is blind. This is undoubtedly the case when the only way to seek a change in the law is by using distraction tactics to slip things into Acts of Parliament covertly. Our laws now spread to the jurisdiction of the Channel Islands, who have a rather peculiar way of obtaining injunctions. Let's just say they do things differently.

In this chapter, we'll learn why the story of Frankenstein's monster is not as make-believe as you were led to believe.

How To Get An Injunction in The Channel Islands

The Channel Islands are a group of British dependency islands just off the Normandy coast of France. There are seven islands in total, Jersey, Guernsey, Alderney, Sark, Herm, Jethou and Brecqhou. The Islands are a lovely place to visit.

In a bizarre but still used ancient law dating back to the tenth century, an islander may seek a temporary legal injunction to prevent someone from wrong-doing by undertaking the *clameur de haro*. This is a call for help to the Duke of Normandy. This has been a legal right of all islanders since the days when they used to call for help from Rollo Rognvaldsson, the first Duke of Normandy (911-927AD). Although, these days, the *clameur* is usually used for matters related to land issues.

One of the earliest documented and famous *clameurs* was that of a landowner named Asselin FitzArthur. He was attending the burial of William the Conqueror. All the bishops and abbots of Normandy were assembled. William's grave was prepared, the mass had just finished, and they were about to lower the King's body into his grave when FitzArthur stepped forward and announced, "*Priests and bishops, this land is mine; it was the site of my father's house; the man for whom you are now praying took it from me by force, to build his church upon it. I have not sold my land; I have not pawned it; I have not forfeited it; I have not given it: it is mine by right, and I demand it. In the name of God, I forbid the body of the spoiler to be placed here, or to be covered with my glebe.*" Members of the congregation confirmed the truthfulness of his statement. Quickly, the bishops approached FitzArthur and agreed to pay him sixty pence for the burial and reimburse him for the rest of his land.

To bring about this injunction, the *criant* (petitioner) must give the *clameur* by going down on one knee, in front of at least two witnesses and preferably also the wrong-doer (defendant). With a hand in the air, they must then cry out in Norman French,

"*Haro! Haro! Haro! À l'aide, mon Prince, on me fait tort.*" (Hear me! Hear me! Hear me! Come to my aid, my Prince, for someone does me wrong) They must then follow this by reciting the Lord's Prayer in French.

Slipping Things Into Acts of Parliament Without Anyone Noticing

Just occasionally, MPs have quietly slipped things into Acts of Parliament, hoping they are overlooked. Once passed, they become law.

Before the passing of The Matrimonial Causes Act (1857), which was the first divorce law enabling people, in general, to apply for a divorce, it was only possible for the wealthy to petition for a divorce. It used to be the case that the church was more powerful than the Crown, and they approved very few divorces. The couple were then permitted to live apart but could not remarry. King Henry VIII paved the way here for us. During the eighteenth and nineteenth centuries, it became possible to get a divorce granted by Act of Parliament. However, this was only available to those with enough money to pay for it and it was expensive.

It was during one such occasion that a local town clerk found himself to be unhappily married. He took the opportunity, whilst promoting a local waterworks Bill at the House of Commons, to secretly insert a special clause of his own into the Bill. And so, according to the story, mixed in amongst all sorts of boring technical jargon about mechanical things and water stopcocks were the words "...*and the Town Clerk's marriage is hereby dissolved...*" This Bill, containing the town clerk's hidden clause, was secretly passed into law.

Treason Was Punishable ... Even After Death

For centuries in England, there was a requirement for the body of any person convicted of treason to be damaged in some way after their execution. Often this would be with beheading or the whole body being chopped into pieces and placed in gibbets around the local town as a warning to other would-be traitors.

It seems similar practices were ever present north of the border in Scotland where a person could be found guilty of treason up to five years after their death.

One of the most well-known cases of a corpse being placed on trial was that of George Gordon, the 4th Earl of Huntly. He was one of the wealthiest and most influential noblemen and owned Huntly Castle in rural Aberdeenshire, Scotland. Unfortunately, he fell out of favour with Mary, Queen of Scots (1542-1567) after her half-brother, the Earl of Moray, became her adviser. In a bizarre turn of events, on 9th October 1562, Mary accused George Gordon of refusing to return a Royal canon lent to him by the Earl of Arran. She immediately ordered Gordon's arrest. He managed to escape in a hurry without wearing any boots, hopped over a low wall at the rear of the castle and rode off on the back of a horse. Infuriated with this, the Queen committed her forces to attack George Gordon. The final showdown occurred at the Battle of Corrichie on 28th October 1562. Huntly was defeated, and Mary's forces seized his castle. The Earl himself died. His eldest son, Sir. John Gordon was executed in Aberdeen. In a rather gruesome spectacle, the Earl's body was embalmed and placed on trial on a charge of treason after his death. We can only imagine the horrible stench of the rotting corpse in the court room, as the charges were put to the lifeless corpse in this elaborate but ludicrously unnecessary trial.

Dr. Frankenstein

For a long time, the bodies of executed criminals were in high demand from the doctors and surgeons of the day. They were needed to practice dissection and other experiments.

One such scientist who desired to experiment on the bodies of the executed was Italian Professor Giovanni Aldini. He was the nephew of the scientist Luigi Galvani, known for his public displays of stimulating muscles with electric current. This became known as Galvanism. This is where the story starts to get interesting because Professor Aldini's next experimental subject was the body of George Foster.

Foster had been found guilty of drowning his wife and youngest son in Paddington Canal, London. He was hanged at Newgate on 18th January 1803. Following this, his body was removed and taken to a nearby house where Professor Aldini conducted his famous 'galvanic process' experiments. During these experiments, Aldini sent bursts of electrical current through Foster's dead body to prove the powers of Galvanism in seemingly bringing a dead body back to life. Several people witnessed this spectacle. Witnesses recounted how Foster's jaw quivered with the first jolt of electricity. Then an eye opened. Then his hand clenched and raised itself, striking a witness, who was left shocked and died that same day, shortly after leaving the experiment.

Many who witnessed this experiment believed Foster was being brought back to life.

When this experiment took place, a young girl called Mary Godwin was just five years old. She had heard much about Galvanism and these experiments at the family dinner table. Her father was a friend of Professor Aldini. Mary soon grew up, and in the summer of 1816, both she and her future husband Percy visited Lord Byron in Geneva, where she was fascinated to hear other stories about Galvanism. Upon marrying Percy, Mary took his surname to become Mary Shelley. In 1818, she released the first edition of her world-famous science-fiction novel 'Frankenstein'.

It is clear that these early experiments on corpses with electricity inspired Mary's novel.

Doli Incapax

These days, children are provided proper legal representation for free. This is one of their rights. Youth Courts now deal with crimes committed by children aged 10 to 17. We no longer have the death penalty or transport offenders to Australia. Although, I'm sure many people would jump at the chance of getting a free ticket to Australia.

It hasn't always been this way.

One of the youngest children executed in England was the 8-year-old John Dean. On 23rd February 1629, he was convicted of arson after setting fire to two houses in Windsor. At the time, the judge, Mr. Justice Whitelock, found evidence of malicious intent and revenge, and this was reflected in his sentencing.

The trial of Mary Wade, aged 13, was held at the Old Bailey on 14th January 1789. Mary used to sweep the streets of London and beg to survive. She was sentenced to death by hanging for stealing a dress, a scarf and a cap from an eight-year-old child. She then sold the dress to a pawnbroker. Luckily for her, this death sentence was dropped. Instead, she was transported to Australia, where she became one of the founding mothers. Amazingly, one of her descendants is former Australian Prime Minister Kevin Rudd.

In 1814, five children were convicted of theft at the Old Bailey, all on the same day. Their ages ranged between 8 years old and 14. Their sentence was death by hanging. In May 1833, 9-year-old Nicholas White was sentenced to death for poking a stick through a cracked shop window and removing 15 tins of paint valued at 2d. This was commuted to a whipping and transportation to Australia for seven years of hard labour.

In August 1845, 8-year-old Thomas Miller was put on trial in Clerkenwell near St. Pancras after being caught "*stealing boxes.*" He was sentenced to one month in jail and whipped. Records also show that a 10-year-old was imprisoned for one month for stealing a hat full of damsons.

The startling question here is how were children this young put on trial, imprisoned or transported, and in some cases executed? This all comes down to the age of criminal responsibility.

Under English common law, the defence of infancy was used. This was called '*Doli Incapax*', which in Latin means that a child under 14 years old is incapable of forming any criminal intent and can not commit an offence. This meant that a child under seven was incapable of committing a crime. It also meant that children aged 7 to 13 were presumed incapable of committing an offence. However, if the prosecution could show that the child understood what they did was wrong, they were allowed to stand trial. Over time, this minimum age gradually changed to reflect society's concerns, later becoming that no child under the age of 10 was capable of committing a crime.

Changes in the law started to occur in 1998.

The current position is that a child under ten years is considered incapable of committing a crime. This is the lowest age of criminal responsibility in Europe.

That means that now, children aged ten and over can be arrested, taken to a police station, interviewed, charged with offences and, if convicted, receive a criminal record.

Interestingly, in Scotland and Ireland, the age of criminal responsibility is 12. Whilst in both Sweden and Denmark, it is 15 years old.

The English Common Law of Deodands

A Deodand is something that is forfeited because it caused death. It dates back to the eleventh century.

During Anglo-Saxon times, whenever death or serious damage was caused by a person's property or their animals, they would have to then hand over the animal or property to the victim or their surviving relatives. Following the Norman Conquest, many of these earlier Anglo-Saxon customs were either lost or altered in some way. This seems to have happened when England transitioned from this ancient system to the law of deodand.

The term is derived from the Latin *'deo dandum'*, which means 'to be given to God'. Under this law, an item of personal property would be handed over as a deodand if it was decided that it had caused the death of a person. This could be anything from a horse, a wagon, a haystack or a myriad of other items of personal property, including animals.

In cases where the property owner could not pay the deodand, the local people would be held responsible for paying the fine to the injured person.

A newspaper article from The Windsor and Eton Express, dated 20th October 1837, refers to a Coroner's inquest into the death of labourer James Stevenson. Mr. Stevenson had died after falling from a cart on Chobham Common. In this sad case, Mr. Stevenson suffered from hearing loss. A person began talking loudly to him so that he could better listen to what they were saying. The horse took this raised voice as a cue to move off. At this point, Mr. Stevenson, standing on the back of the cart, lost his balance and fell off, banging his head on the ground. The attending doctor gave the cause of death as a violent concussion of the brain. The jury returned a verdict of *"Accidental death, with a deodand of one shilling on the horse."*

Keep It In The Family

When someone coined the phrase 'keep it in the family', I don't think this is quite what they had in mind. An ancient Anglo-Saxon law later abolished by King Canute (1016–1035) dealt with stolen property. If stolen property was found in a house, and an occupant of that house was named the thief, his wife and the whole family, including the infant in the cradle, were all punished equally as though they were guilty.

It wasn't just the humans in the household that would be found guilty. Other Anglo-Saxon laws treated all domestic animals in a house as accessories in crimes of violence. All those animals would then be sentenced to death.

Blood Feud

The Anglo-Saxon Kings allowed the victims of crime to punish the criminals themselves. This system became known as '*Blood feud*' and focused heavily on retaliation as a form of sentencing. For the more serious offences, for example, murder, the idea of imprisoning murderers hadn't even been considered. Instead, the Kings allowed retribution through blood feuds. Where a person had been murdered, the closest next-of-kin was permitted to track down and kill the murderer.

This ancient punishment system wasn't a complete bloodbath. There were strict rules to be followed. The severity of the crime committed led to the method of punishment, which, more often than not, was through compensation. There were other rules as well governing blood feuds. If the person murdered was themself a convicted thief, then a blood feud was not permitted.

Blood feuds continued until just after the Norman Conquest of 1066.

Wergild

This alternative form of compensation for a crime was based on a system of fines paid to the victims of crime or their families. This was known as '*Wergild*'. This literally translated as 'man-price'. This system was based on a monetary value established as compensation to the victim's family for the loss of life.

This system of compensation was unfairly unequal, and the level of fine (Wergild) depended on the victim's social standing. For example, the highest fine was for the killing of the King or a Lord. The Wergild paid for the killing of a nobleman was 300 shillings, whereas the Wergild for the death of a freeman was 100 shillings. The murder of a peasant or a slave was considerably lower. Lower still was the Wergild that had to be paid for killing a Welshman.

Interestingly, the Wergild for a woman was more than for a man and could often be twice as much as that given for a man.

The law started to regulate how much compensation (Wergild) would be paid for each body part lost or injured. A severed nose was 60 shillings, an eye fetched 50 shillings, an ear cut off was 30 shillings, 20 shillings for a big toe, 9 shillings for a little finger, and the victim of a broken arm would only receive 6 shillings.

Magna Carta

The Magna Carta, one of the most famous documents in the world, arguably forms the basis of English law and certainly the foundations of the criminal justice system.

This Charter set out the laws that every person, including The King, had to follow in 63 clauses. It stated that every person was subject to the law and nobody was above it. Essentially, it was the earliest form of the rule of law. It was considered so important that, at the time, copies were sent out to every county in England to ensure everyone knew of its existence and the laws.

Today, only four original copies of the Magna Carta survive. Two are kept in the British Library, one is at Lincoln Castle, and the fourth is on display at Salisbury Cathedral. The Magna Carta enjoyed its 800th anniversary on 15th June 2015.

Although commonly called the Magna Carta, its full title is the *'Magna Carta Libertatum'*, which in mediaeval Latin stands for the 'Great Charter of Freedoms'.

King John of England granted this early Royal Charter on 15th June 1215 at Runnymede, a water meadow on the banks of the River Thames near Windsor. The King knew that many powerful barons in England were looking to overthrow him, so this first draft of the Magna Carta in 1215 was more about the King making peace by giving up some of his power to the rebel barons. It took away some of the King's authority and provided protection for the church, access to justice and protection from illegal imprisonment (especially for the barons). As it happened, neither The King nor the barons adhered to their commitments. This first Charter was annulled by Pope Innocent III just ten weeks later, making it no longer valid.

The Magna Carta remained untouched until in 1828, one of the clauses was repealed.

During the reign of Queen Victoria, we saw the most significant number of changes to the Magna Carta. This started in 1863, when 17 clauses were repealed. These were considered obsolete and mainly related to mediaeval things that had become outdated. A further six clauses were repealed before the end of Queen Victoria's reign.

In 1969, a further six clauses were repealed from the Magna Carta, including the bizarre Clause 23, which entitled townsmen and freemen to build as many bridges over rivers as they like and wherever they want.

This brings us into the 21st century, where much of the original Magna Carta has long since been chipped away, with just three clauses remaining on the statute books in England and Wales. These relate to the freedom of the English church, the "*ancient liberties*" of the City of London, and very importantly, the right to due legal process.

Clauses 39 & 40 relate to the Right to Trial by Jury. It states,

"*No free man shall be seized or imprisoned, or stripped of his rights or possessions, or outlawed or exiled, or deprived of his standing in any other way, nor will we proceed with force against him, or send others to do so, except by the lawful judgement of his equals or by the law of the land. To no one will we sell, to no one will we deny or delay right or justice.*"

Habeas Corpus

Habeas Corpus is an Act of Parliament which still exists today. It is taken from the mediaeval Latin phrase '*Habeas corpus ad subjiciendum*', which means 'Let the body be brought before the judge'. It ensures that no-one can be unlawfully imprisoned by requiring that a prisoner is produced in person at a court when a person reports that an unlawful detention has occurred. The court will then determine whether the prisoner's custody is lawful.

The basic idea of *habeas corpus* originates from a law passed in 1166, during King Henry II's reign, leading to trials by jury. King John's 1215 Magna Carta stated that no-one could be unlawfully imprisoned. The Act came about as a result of an unimaginable set of circumstances which caused such a public outcry at the time it was felt necessary that some action be taken to ensure such an occurrence never again happens.

The circumstances to which I refer are the drinking habits of a particular lady called Alice Robinson. One night in 1621, Mrs. Robinson and her husband were hosting a private party at their home in High Holborn, London. The party could only be described as a rowdy and drunken occasion; although, I imagine, nothing that would raise an eyebrow these days. On this occasion, a passing constable overheard what he described as *"a brawling, fighting noise."* So, he entered their home to investigate further. He later gave an account in court stating that once inside the address, he witnessed *"men and women in disordered and uncivil accompanying together"* ... again, nothing out of the ordinary in today's society. The constable accused Mrs. Robinson of causing a disturbance in her neighbourhood. She swore at the constable and was arrested and imprisoned in the Clerkenwell House of Correction.

Whilst imprisoned, Mrs. Robinson's party guests were petitioning for her release. After a while, she was brought before the Old Bailey for the case to be heard. The court and Mrs. Robinson's friends, many of whom were influential, were utterly shocked to hear of her experience in the House of Correction. She alleged that she was forced to sleep on bare earth and given nothing but water and black bread. This was considered harsh even by prison standards in those days. She went on to tell how she had been stripped naked and given 50 lashes with the whip. When finally, she revealed that she was also pregnant whilst all this was going on, there was an outcry. The jury immediately found her not guilty and the constable who had arrested her, then found himself imprisoned in Newgate Prison for arresting her without a warrant. The local justice of the peace, who had earlier signed a warrant for her detention in the Clerkenwell House of Correction, was also given a strong telling off.

This provoked the Earl of Shaftesbury to encourage several of his friends to introduce a Bill in the House of Commons. During voting on the Bill, people were appointed to keep count of the 'Aye' votes and the 'Nay' votes. The tellers each stood by a door to count the votes as the parliamentarians entered. One teller would count aloud each person as they entered, whilst the other teller listened and ensured there was no wrong-doing. Gilbert Burnet, the Bishop of Salisbury, noted some of the events from that fateful vote. He wrote, *"Lord Grey and Lord Norris were named to be the tellers: Lord Norris ... was not at all times attentive to what he was doing: so, a very fat lord coming in, Lord Grey counted him as ten, as a jest at first: but seeing Lord Norris had not observed it, he went on with this misreckoning of ten: so it was reported that they that were for the Bill were in the majority, though indeed it went for the other side: and by this means the Bill passed."*

Despite this, the clerk nevertheless recorded in the minutes that the 'Ayes' had 57 votes and the 'Nays' had only 55 votes. This totalled 112 votes. However, the same record also documented that there were only 107 Lords present during that sitting. After noticing this, Lord Shaftesbury immediately rose to his feet and spoke for almost one hour, discussing various matters. During this time, several peers had entered or left the House, making any recount an impossibility. Shortly afterwards, The King arrived and gave his Royal Assent to the Bill, giving us The Habeas Corpus Act (1679), which still exists today.

The Great Seal

The Great Seal of the Realm is used on all important State documents to show the Sovereign's approval. During the reign of King Edward the Confessor (1042-1066), he began to use a double-sided 'Great Seal' which was cast in metal. This was used to make a wax image of The King's face as an official Seal on documents to show his approval. A ribbon would also be attached under the wax. The Seal meant that the King no longer needed to sign every official document, and his endorsement could be carried out using the Great Seal by another person, known as The Keeper of the Great Seal. Since 1761, this office has been held jointly with the office of the Lord Chancellor. They are now the same person.

Even today, whilst the Sovereign generally acts upon the advice of his government, this Seal remains a significant symbol of the Sovereign's authority as Head of State.

The Great Seal has suffered some mishaps over the centuries, and some Lord Chancellors have been very protective over the safe custody of the Seal. Lord Chancellor Heneage Finch, 1st Earl of Nottingham, was known to take the Great Seal to bed with him. On one occasion, this unusual sleeping habit paid off when on 7th February 1677, his house in Queen Street was burgled. At around 1am, the burglar, Thomas Sadler, stole the ceremonial silver mace worth £100 and two velvet purses embroidered with gold and silver encrusted with pearls worth £40 but could not steal the Great Seal as it was tucked safely under the Lord Chancellor's pillow. Sadler and his co-conspirator returned to their house carrying the mace on his shoulder. They then stuck their loot in a cupboard which was later discovered by their landlady whilst cleaning. They were both arrested and later hanged at Tyburn on 16th March 1677.

On 10th December 1688, King James II dropped the Great Seal in the River Thames whilst attempting to flee to France. He believed that any new government could not legally pass any laws without it. However, it is believed that it was caught in a fisherman's net in Lambeth and later returned.

The Great Seal suffered yet another mishap on 24th March 1784. It was stolen from the Lord Chancellor Lord Thurlow's house in Great Ormond Street, London, on the night before the dissolution of Parliament. The burglars climbed over his garden wall and forcibly removed two iron bars from his kitchen window. It is clear the burglars knew in advance of the location of the Seal because they went straight to his study and broke open the lock on the writing table drawer. The thieves were caught, but unfortunately, the Great Seal, made from silver, had already been melted down. This severely delayed Parliamentary business, and a Cabinet Council meeting was immediately called to order that a new Seal be quickly made.

Chapter Thirteen

Money

They say that money is the root of all evil.

Once you've read this chapter, you may be inclined to agree with that statement. There have certainly been enough laws created on our statute books for money-related offences.

There is a Limit to How Many Coins You Can Legally Use

All coins minted by the Royal Mint and authorised by Royal Proclamation are legal tender in England, Scotland, Wales and Northern Ireland. The law states which denomination of coins are legal tender and to what value they may be used in any single transaction. According to the law, 1p and 2p coins are legal tender in the UK only up to an amount not exceeding 20 pence if used in the same transaction. There is an exception. You can use more 1p and 2p coins if the person you're paying is happy to accept them.

In fact, there are also stipulations for 5p, 10p, 20p and 50p coins.

The maximum amounts for which coins are accepted as legal tender in the UK are as follows:

- For £2 and £1 coins: any amount
- For 50p and 20p coins: up to £10
- For 10p and 5p coins: up to £5
- For 2p and 1p coins: up to 20 pence

You may be interested to know that coins remain legal tender irrespective of how they are presented ... even if they are in a block of ice or a bucket of rice pudding.

There are stories in the newspapers of people trying to pay their parking fines with bucket loads of pennies.

Illegal to Deface a Banknote But Not Illegal to Destroy It

It is an offence to deface a banknote by printing, stamping or writing any words, letters or figures on it.

However, whilst it is an offence to deface a banknote, it is not an offence to wilfully destroy a banknote. Quite why you would want to do that, I have no idea ... unless you're trying to hide some evidence of a bank robbery!

It is also an offence to destroy a metal coin that has been in circulation in the UK since 1969. In 2017, the Royal Mint had to issue a reminder to the general public when it became apparent that people were deliberately disassembling the new £1 coins and separating them into the two separate parts of the inner circle and outer circle and then fixing them back together, the wrong way around. These were being sold on eBay. Understandably the Royal Mint were unhappy and issued a reminder that deliberately manipulating coins in this way was an offence.

The Sovereign's Image on Coins Faces The Opposite Direction For Each New Reign

From the start of King Charles III's reign, all the coins in circulation would gradually be replaced with new ones depicting the new Sovereign's image. These would replace the 29 billion coins currently in general circulation, displaying Her late Majesty's image. When The Royal Mint revealed the new coins, this startling difference surprised many. The King is facing the opposite direction to his mother.

Not only is the King not wearing a crown, but he is facing towards the left. His mother, the late Queen, faced towards the right. This is part of a tradition that has lasted since the seventeenth century. The Queen's father, King George VI, faced in the opposite direction on coins, towards the left. The recent convention is that male Sovereigns don't wear crowns in their image. Female Sovereigns wear a crown or tiara and can accessorise with jewellery.

Every monarch from the time of King Charles II has alternated the direction they face on our coins. That is, except for the monarch who liked to rebel against convention, King Edward VIII. He chose to break with tradition because he preferred portraits of him facing towards the left, which he felt presented his better side.

His younger brother, Prince Albert, was next in line to the throne and became King George VI. He restored the tradition. It was considered preferable for the image of King George VI to face towards the left on coins to maintain the continuity of the tradition, as though the image of King Edward VIII had, in fact, been placed towards the right during his brief reign.

King Henry VIII Debased His Own Currency to Profit From The People

By the mid-sixteenth century, Henry VIII had overspent to fund his lavish lifestyle and wars with France and Scotland. In May 1542, King Henry VIII devised a cunning plan. He ordered the Royal Mint to secretly reduce the amount of gold and silver in the coins they made. These precious metals were replaced (debased) with cheaper base metals, like copper. As a result, between 1544 and 1551, both King Henry VIII and his son, King Edward VI, gradually reduced the content of the nation's silver coins from 92.5% sterling silver to just 25%. Silver coins issued in 1551 contained only 17% sterling silver. This was the same with gold coins.

MONEY 177

The country noticed this difference, especially when Henry VIII started issuing his previously stockpiled Testoons (shilling coins). These had been covered thinly in a silver layer to hide the underlying cheaper copper. This thin layer of silver tended to rub off. It was particularly noticeable over the Kings protruding nose on the coin. This revealed the high copper content of the coins and earned the King the nickname 'Old Coppernose'.

When Queen Elizabeth I came to power in 1558, she immediately passed a law prohibiting all good coins from leaving the country and quickly removed all the debased coins from general circulation. By 1560, around 90% of the coins in circulation had been removed and re-minted, restoring confidence in English money.

Chapter Fourteen

PARLIAMENT

The Houses of Parliament are located in the Palace of Westminster in London. They are responsible for passing our laws and holding the government accountable. They have been an essential feature of the British political landscape as the seat of democracy since the thirteenth century.

Incredibly we have such events in our history as The Gunpowder Plot, where Guy Fawkes and his conspirators tried to blow up Parliament and kill The King. For centuries after, we were legally required to celebrate the death of Guy Fawkes each year on the 5th of November.

The walls of that hallowed place where new laws are passed are steeped in history and other bizarre goings-on. It is no wonder each newly elected Speaker has to be forcefully dragged to his chair.

You Can't Die in The Houses of Parliament

Politics isn't everyone's cup of tea. In fact, for some, the mere thought of it bores them to death. But that's okay just as long as they don't die in the Houses of Parliament. Whilst it is not an offence to die in the Houses of Parliament, no-one is allowed to die there. There is a good reason behind this. The Palace of Westminster is a Royal palace, and no person can be declared dead on the estate except for the Royal family. There is a myth that the reason behind this is that anyone who dies in a Royal palace is entitled to a State funeral. This is not the case. If it were, any tourists visiting the many Royal palaces around the UK, including Hampton Court and The Tower of London, would also be entitled to a State funeral should they choose to die there.

So, what happens if a visitor on a House of Commons tour suffers the inconvenience of a heart attack and dies in the building? Under these circumstances, their body would be removed from the Parliamentary estate and their death certificate is issued at St Thomas' Hospital in Lambeth, just over Westminster Bridge.

This goes back to a law passed by King Henry VIII in 1541.

MPs Not Allowed to Carry Nunchucks or Wear Armour in Parliament

According to an ancient law, no-one is permitted to bring weapons of any sort or to wear armour in the Houses of Parliament. This law doesn't just cover MPs; it covers any person on the Parliamentary estate.

This law was passed by King Edward II in 1313. By this time, the King had reigned for six years and had already upset many of the powerful land barons. Different groups of barons jostled for power and to control the King. To prevent barons from turning up to Parliament dressed in full armour and carrying swords, he decided to pass this law to prevent threats against him inside Parliament.

There is one exception to the carrying of weapons. The Serjeant at Arms is allowed to carry a sword, as is Black Rod, when entering the Chamber to summon MPs to hear the King's speech.

Mr. Speaker

With 650 Members of Parliament elected in the House of Commons, that's a lot of voices, high-volume and arguments during the many regular debates held daily in the House of Commons Chamber. There is, of course, the rulebook called Erskine May that all MPs follow, but there still needs to be a person who controls the proceedings, a sort of chairperson. This is the role of the Speaker of the House of Commons, more commonly known as Mr. Speaker. Every question, statement or point of order raised by an MP in the House of Commons must be directed through The Speaker. This ensures proceedings remain civil and don't spiral out of control into a shouting match or arguments.

The Speaker ultimately controls the House and decides what amendments are selected, who speaks and in what order. MPs have the right to have their voices heard in the Chamber, and at times that necessitates Mr. Speaker gently reminding the Members of The House of the rules. The Speaker has the authority to discipline and pass summary sentences for minor transgressions in the Chamber, for example, where one MP says bad things about another and refuses to withdraw their comments. The Speaker may then punish the offending MP by 'naming' them and suspending them from Parliament for the day.

The office of The Speaker is an interesting role, almost as old as Parliament itself. The earliest recorded chair of proceedings in a Parliament is the presiding officer Peter de Montfort in 1258. It was the Parliament held in Oxford. The title of Speaker can be traced back to 1376 when Sir Peter de la Mare held it.

The Speaker is Dragged to His Chair

Some days you wake up and feel like going back to sleep again. You almost have to be dragged out of bed. Some people actually do get physically dragged to work. In a curious centuries-old custom, when a new Speaker of the House of Commons is elected, the successful MP is ceremoniously dragged by other MPs from his seat to the Speaker's chair. The Speaker feigns reluctance as they are dragged to their chair.

Historically, it was The Speaker's role to communicate between The House of Commons and the Sovereign. There were times when the Sovereign wasn't too happy with the goings-on in Parliament or with the messages being conveyed, resulting in punishment or death for The Speaker. As you can imagine, an MP would have been reluctant to be elected as The Speaker; hence, why they have to be physically dragged to The Speaker's chair. Over the centuries, several Speakers have been executed for displeasing the Sovereign.

On 4th November 2019, Sir. Lindsay Hoyle, became the latest Speaker of The House, and was dragged to The Speaker's Chair in this elaborate ceremony.

The House of Commons Has a Father and a Mother

The House of Commons is like one large family, complete with its regular internal squabbling and fallings out.

As with many families, there is a father and a mother. The *'Father of The House'* is the longest continuously serving male MP at that time. It is the same for the *'Mother of The House'*, being the longest continuously serving female MP.

Records show that the longest-serving Father of The House was Winston Churchill. Although his service was not continuous. He was first elected on 1st October 1900 and left the House of Commons on 25th September 1964, 63 years and 360 days later. Sadly, he died just four months after leaving. Before that, Francis Knollys, MP for Oxford and Reading, was elected in 1575 and continued in office for 73 years until he died in 1648. However, during his time as an MP, Parliament didn't meet for 27 years.

If there were a title of *'Baby of The House'*, that would have to go to the MP for Devon, Christopher Monck, who was elected in 1667 at just 13 years old. He sat as an MP for three years.

Legally Required to Celebrate the Death of Guy Fawkes

Each year, the USA celebrates thanksgiving. We have our own thanksgiving. It's called The Observance of 5th November Act (1605), also known as the Thanksgiving Act. It was a law passed in 1606 in the aftermath of the Gunpowder Plot when Guy Fawkes was caught trying to blow up Parliament and kill King James I. The law required that the public celebrate thanksgiving on the 5th November each year to celebrate "*with unfeigned thankfulness*" the capture and execution of Guy Fawkes.

Every person had to attend their parish church or a chapel to pray and mark this event on 5th November.

This law was repealed during Queen Victoria's reign on 25th March 1859. These days, whilst it is no longer a legal requirement to celebrate the capture and death of Guy Fawkes and his co-conspirators, we nevertheless choose to celebrate each year with large bonfires and firework displays.

Penny for The Guy

Whilst it is now more of a dying tradition, each year, in certain places around the UK, groups of children will sit outside supermarkets or go door-to-door with a stuffed dummy of Guy Fawkes, collecting 'a Penny for the Guy'.

Guy Fawkes failed to blow up King James I and Parliament on 5th November 1605. He was discovered the night before and captured. He was held at the Tower of London where, under torture, he revealed the names of his co-conspirators in the Gunpowder Plot. He was sentenced to be hanged, drawn and quartered for his crimes.

Penny for the Guy used to be very popular. The children would collect money which would then be handed over to buy the fireworks for the whole community to enjoy on 5th November.

The Guy would often be a life-sized dummy made from old coats and rags, stuffed with straw or old newspaper. The Guy's head would be made from either papier-mâché or an old pair of tights. Children used to stuff their Guy into a wheelbarrow, pushchair or even a shopping trolley and push them around the streets, shouting 'Penny for the Guy!'

Police officers see Penny for the Guy as a form of mischief, public nuisance and begging. When antisocial behaviour laws were introduced in the early 2000s, this provided the police with further rules to enforce against children. The police have even set up 'nuisance patrols' to target children collecting cash with their Guy Fawkes dummy. It is not in the public's interest to punish children for these offences. So, the police usually just move the children along to somewhere else.

Since 1824, collecting money on the streets or even going door-to-door is considered begging.

Each Year The Cellars of Parliament Are Searched For Barrels of Gunpowder

Each year on the eve before the State Opening of Parliament, His Majesty's Yeoman of the Guard diligently search the cellars of the Houses of Parliament, looking for barrels of gunpowder. They quietly walk through the building and the cellars, each guard carrying a storm lantern. This is part of an ancient ceremony dating back to the reign of King James I and the nasty incident of the Gunpowder Plot led by Guy Fawkes.

A brief history lesson... In 1604, Guy Fawkes and a group of Catholics, led by Robert Catesby, decided it would be a good idea to assassinate the Protestant King James I whilst he attended The House of Lords. They planned to kill the King, kidnap his nine-year-old daughter Princess Elizabeth and convert her to Catholicism. The plot was discovered when an anonymous letter was sent to William Parker, 4th Baron Monteagle and the authorities were alerted. A subsequent search of the Parliament cellars found Guy Fawkes stood guarding a pile of wood near 36 barrels of gunpowder. This led to today's annual searching of the cellars on the eve before the State Opening of Parliament.

Following their search of the cellars, the Yeoman of the Guard are each provided with half a glass of Port to drink.

The King Holds a Member of Parliament Prisoner Once a Year

Each year, at the State Opening of Parliament, the King sits on his throne in the House of Lords and delivers his speech. He outlines the plans of his government for the next year. On the same morning, the King holds a Member of Parliament hostage ... and everyone is okay with it. This is a centuries-old tradition dating back to the time of the Stuarts when King Charles I and Parliament had a poor relationship, which eventually led to the King being executed in 1649.

The purpose behind the Royal household taking a Member of Parliament hostage is to ensure the safe passage and return of His Majesty following the State Opening of Parliament. It is said that if any harm befalls His Majesty whilst on Parliamentary estate, the same fate will befall the Member of Parliament.

They are kept at Buckingham Palace until the Monarch safely returns. The 'hostage' in 2022 was the Conservative MP James Morris, who was met by the Lord Chamberlain.

In 2014, the hostage was the Labour MP, Jim Fitzpatrick. He recalled his time at The Palace as a hostage. He stated that the Lord Chamberlain clarified that he was more of a guest and could do whatever he wanted at Buckingham Palace. He could wander around freely and have a drink or other refreshments. Instead, he chose to sit and watch the State Opening on television. They did make it clear that he wasn't allowed to leave the Palace grounds. He expressed his anxiety to the Chief of the Defence Staff, who told him, *"If anything happened to Her Majesty, Jim, we would have made it quick. We would have just shot you."* He was, of course, joking.

Chapter Fifteen

POLICE

Constables have been around since the sixth century, but it wasn't until the creation of the modern-day police force in 1829 that we started to see consistency in how police constables operated in different counties. That hasn't always been a good thing.

His Majesty's finest, the British police, enforce the laws passed for centuries by Parliament. We are in an eternal love-hate relationship with them. Like them or loathe them, they are the ones who uphold the law and bring offenders to justice.

In this chapter, we'll examine why the police have to pay for mass public disturbances, the public doesn't have to talk to them ... and why they're always on duty!

The Police Have to Pay For All Property Damaged, Destroyed or Stolen During Riots

When we talk about riots, we imagine widespread disorder with hundreds and thousands of people protesting about something, with shops being damaged or looted and cars set on fire. For a riot to occur, in law, it doesn't need thousands of people, only 12 or more. That describes almost every Friday and Saturday night outside pubs and nightclubs in most major UK cities. It also describes occurrences at most major sporting events.

During these riots, widespread disorder and mass damage can be caused to businesses, shops and even people's homes. So, who ends up paying for all of the damage? Is it the individual home and business owner? This question was answered in 1886 with the passing of The Riot (Damages) Act. This Victorian law required local police authorities to pay for any damage, destruction, or thefts occurring during a riot. The police authority had to pay this compensation to victims of these riot-related crimes, irrespective of whether the police force had been negligent.

These days, many insurance policies covering shops and houses do not cover loss, damage or destruction caused by rioting due to the expectation that the local police authority will pay as ordered under this 1886 law.

Lying To The Police

There are some occasions when you are required by law to speak to the police, and it is important that you do not lie. Whilst there is no actual offence of lying to the police, that does not make it illegal. You may commit one or more serious offences depending on the circumstances in which you find yourself speaking to a police officer, if you choose to lie.

The whole criminal justice system is based on the foundations of honesty and integrity. Imagine if everyone lied to the police and the courts. There would be guilty people walking free and innocent people being imprisoned. Before the death penalty was abolished, this would have meant innocent people would have been handed the death sentence. This has happened on occasion and continues to happen to this day, which is why laws must exist to prevent lying to the police and the courts and ensure justice is rightly served.

If in doubt, don't say anything at all. Exercise your legal right not to incriminate yourself. Other than on very few occasions, you aren't actually required to say anything to a police officer.

There are several offences for which lying to the police can end up with you in hot water. The first is what is commonly referred to as the offence of '*Wasting police time*'. This offence generally occurs when a person makes a false report to the police. It carries a maximum penalty of six months imprisonment. Offenders may be given a fine. This offence can be committed even if a false report is made to someone other than a police officer, provided that the other person brings it to the attention of the police and it subsequently wastes police time. You also have to knowingly provide a false report for this offence to be committed.

An example of this could be telling a police officer that you've heard screams and shouting coming from an address. The police officer, after ringing the doorbell for several minutes, is concerned for the safety of the people within. He then kicks the back door in, only to discover there is actually no-one inside the address. He turns around and sees you laughing. You have made a false report leading the police officer to fear for the safety of the people within the house.

There is a significant overlap between this offence and another offence under common law called *'Perverting the Course of Justice'*. This is a much more severe offence with a maximum sentence of life imprisonment.

So, let's say the false report you initially made to the police has the consequence of not just wasting a few hours of police time but also leading to a large-scale police investigation involving many police officers and resulting in a person being wrongly arrested. In this case, the Crown Prosecution Service (CPS) may decide to charge you with this more serious offence of Perverting the Course of Justice.

This leads us to the next offence related to lying, 'Perjury'. Once lawfully sworn in as a witness in court, if a person knowingly makes a statement which they know is a lie or do not believe it to be true, they commit this offence. The maximum sentence for perjury is seven years imprisonment. You can understand why this offence is so important. If a witness makes a false statement in court, it can lead to an innocent person being found guilty or vice versa.

With all this said, I'll remind you again that under most circumstances, there is no legal obligation to talk to a police officer. If you do, it really doesn't pay to lie.

All Police Officers Are Constables, Irrespective of Their Rank

Many of you will be familiar with the police rank structure, perhaps from being immersed in policing and detective dramas on television and watching films. Police officers will start their careers in the rank of Constable. The next rank is Sergeant, followed by Inspector and Chief Inspector. This moves up to the chief officer of the force, usually a Chief Constable or the Commissioner of the Metropolitan Police Service.

On appointment, each police officer and special constable (unpaid volunteer police officers) is required by law to take the attestation oath, making a declaration in front of a justice of the peace, usually during an attestation ceremony.

Each officer derives their powers from the ancient Office of Constable. This office provides police officers with their additional legal powers of arrest as servants of the Crown.

Historically, we know that the Office of Constable existed during the reign of King Henry I (1100-1135). Like many of the roles of that time, their duties were primarily concerned with military matters. It was most likely introduced following the Norman conquest.

The 1285 Statute of Westminster, passed by King Edward I, refers to two high constables appointed for every hundred citizens to suppress uprisings and ensure the adequate arming of the local militia.

The Office of Constable remained this way, acting as a servant to the Crown for centuries. It wasn't until just before the Victorian era that we started to see the birth of modern-day policing. In 1829, the then Home Secretary Sir. Robert Peel established the London Metropolitan Police Force. This is why British police are sometimes known as 'Bobbies', Bob being the nickname for Robert (Peel) or 'Peelers'.

Interestingly, irrespective of their rank, still to this day, all police officers, from Constable right up to Chief Constable, are nevertheless all Constables.

A Police Officer is Always On Duty

Unlike most other jobs, the police officer may punch a timecard or sign out on a computerised system at the end of their shift. However, they are not able to just switch off their duties under their Office of Constable. The truth is that police officers may bring themselves on duty at any time. Their powers are derived from their sworn Office of Constable, and this doesn't stop just because they step into the shower or go out shopping at the local supermarket.

This doesn't mean that police officers are permitted to walk around while off-duty, wearing their full uniform. If they did and were carrying a baton, CS incapacitant spray or their Taser, they would be guilty of multiple crimes. Although interestingly, it is not an offence to carry handcuffs around in public.

No General Law Requiring You to Talk to a Police Officer

In the UK, if you haven't committed an offence and you're not suspected of having committed an offence, with very few exceptions, there is no legal requirement for you to talk to a police officer. Although, why would you not? They are, after all, members of the public just like you and me. It is perfectly acceptable to talk to police officers, and I'm sure the majority of them don't bite. It becomes slightly different if they suspect you have committed an offence and wish to ask you questions about that. As soon as a police officer suspects you of an offence, they are required by law, to first caution you before asking you any questions about that offence. Failure to do so can render anything you say to them inadmissible in evidence.

The wording of the police caution is, "*You do not have to say anything. But it may harm your defence if you do not mention when questioned something which you later rely on in court. Anything you do say may be given in evidence.*" This same caution has to be given to any person suspected of an offence, including minor motoring offences if the police officer wishes to ask you questions specifically about that offence.

You are entitled to various rights before you answer any questions, and these are things like a right to speak to a solicitor, for free. Even during voluntary police interviews, you are entitled to free legal advice from a solicitor. There is no need to answer any police questions until you have received that legal advice. Police officers must also inform you of these rights before they ask you questions in relation to a suspected offence.

I'll reiterate that there is no legal obligation to talk to a police officer, even if they walk over to you in the street to speak to you. It can be intimidating at times to talk to the police. If you wish to walk away, you are perfectly within your rights to do so. If the police suspect you have committed an offence, then they do have the power to stop you from walking away. If you are being detained, it must be either for the purpose of a stop and search or an arrest. If it is not, you can simply decline to have a conversation and walk away. Even if the police are stopping you to conduct a search, you are still not required to provide your details or even talk to them.

If you do talk to the police, especially under caution, you mustn't lie. If you do, this could be an offence in itself. There are certain occasions when the police can require you, by law, to talk to them. Even in these circumstances, they are limited in what they can ask you. For example, if the police suspect you have committed an offence and state that they require you to provide your name and address for the service of a summons, then you should provide those details. If you fail to do so, they can arrest you to establish your identification at the police station.

There are laws that deal with anti-social behaviour. It provides police with the legal power to demand your name and address if they believe you are or have been acting in an anti-social manner. This is any form of behaviour that is likely to cause "*harassment, alarm or distress*" to another member of the public. This is one of those circumstances when you must provide your name and address. It is an offence to refuse to do so or to provide false information. It only requires you to provide your name and address and no further details.

The Police Can Not Detain You Without Arrest

On many occasions, police officers will stop members of the public to enquire who they are, where they're from, and what they're doing. As you'll see elsewhere in this chapter, with very few exceptions, you are under no legal obligation to stop and talk to the police or answer any of their questions. These are your fundamental human rights. Sometimes, police officers will try to detain a person whilst working out what has occurred and whether they should formally arrest that person. However, with very few exceptions, the police have no such power.

A police officer may physically detain a person on the streets or otherwise impede their movements only in limited circumstances where they are not making an arrest. The first instance is where police officers use their powers of Stop and Search. This could be, for example, to search a person if they have reasonable grounds for *suspecting* that they will find stolen or prohibited articles such as a weapon, stolen property, prohibited fireworks, or something that could be used to commit a crime. Any detention may only last for as long as it reasonably requires to undertake the search. During the search, the officer may ask you for some details like your name, address, date of birth, whether you are "*known to the police*," what you are up to, where you are going, etc. You DO NOT have to give this information to the police officer unless they point out that an offence has been committed and they suspect your involvement in that offence. In this case, you may provide your name and address only, remind them of their obligation to first caution you before asking any further questions and request your entitlement to speak to a solicitor before you answer any further questions.

Another occasion where a police officer may lawfully detain a person without arrest is where it is necessary to temporarily restrain or detain a person to prevent a breach of the peace from happening in the immediate future.

So, to recap, a police officer has no additional power over any other member of the public to detain a person on the streets without arrest unless under those few circumstances. Detention does not need to be physical. It could merely be an officer standing in your way to prevent you from moving.

If an officer decides to detain you without this lawful authority, this will constitute an *Assault and Battery*. This is the case even if no injury is caused to you.

If a police officer asks you to sit in the back of their car whilst they ask you some questions, and you agree, you may withdraw that permission at any time by telling the officer that you no longer consent to be held in the back of their vehicle and wish to leave. If the officer continues to detain you without arresting you, they would be committing an offence of *False Imprisonment*. Being kept against your will in the back of a police vehicle and with no legal power to do so is no different from being placed in handcuffs or in a cell at a police station. Your freedom has been taken away.

Chapter Sixteen
Punishment & Torture

We've all heard about the harsh punishments of the Victorian age. Victorian schools were a particularly hostile environment for any child to find themselves. Those who stepped on the wrong side of the law in Victorian society could find themselves thrown into prison and forced to undergo hard, repetitive and boring labour. Some prisoners found this punishment so harsh they literally dropped dead.

In this chapter, we peer into the macabre world of gruesome punishments and inhumane torture methods. We examine the reasons behind each of them, the laws that allowed them to take place and some notable recipients throughout the centuries. Surprisingly, at least one form of punishment you will read about still exists in our statute books.

Victorian Classroom Punishments

Life in Victorian schools was harsh, and punishments were unforgiving. Children were frequently caned. The canes were made from birch wood. Boys would be caned on the bottom, while girls were caned across the palms of their hands or on the back of their legs. Children could receive a caning for something as simple as being lazy, lying, poor attendance, insolence, or just leaving a classroom without permission. In Scotland, a leather strap called a tawse was used instead of the cane. A running log of punishments was kept in the school punishments book.

Those children caught fidgeting in lessons, would have their hands tied behind their backs, or their fingers could be placed in small wooden finger stocks. Children unable to answer questions or those considered 'slow' would be forced to wear a pointed Dunce hat with the letter 'D' on it. They would then have to stand in the corner of the classroom for an hour or more. Children caught slouching in lessons would have a rigid wooden backboard shoved down their back to force them to sit up straight. Left-handed children caught trying to write with their left hands would quickly find them tied down, and they were forced to continue writing with their right hand. If any of this upset a child and they cried, they would be further punished for crying.

Some of the strict rules that applied in Victorian classrooms were as follows:

1. Students must stand up to answer questions and wait for permission to speak

2. Students must call teachers '*Sir*', '*Miss*' or '*Mrs*'

3. Students must stand when an adult enters the room

4. Students must use the right hand at all times for writing

5. Girls will learn needlework, and boys will learn technical drawing

6. Students must not put their hands up until told they can do so

7. Students must not ask questions

8. Talking and fidgeting will be punished

9. Children who are truant (late), behave badly or do poor work will be caned

Severing of The Foot

All sorts of gruesome punishments used to be given to those who committed offences. This could even be for something as small as taking a loaf of bread. The offender would have his foot cut clean off in one such punishment. This would be instead of the sentence of death. It was considered that letting a man live but inconvenienced and crippled in hardship for the rest of his life was far better than a sentence of death, which would provide little relief for the victims of crime.

This particular method of punishment came over to our shores with the invasion of William the Conqueror. In one of his early laws, it stated, "*We forbid that anyone should be killed or hanged for any crime, but that the eyes should be bled, the feet, or the testicles, or the hands should be cut off.*"

What a lovely chap!

Branding

Branding, as a form of punishment, first came into use during Anglo-Saxon times and continued into nineteenth-century Britain. Long before the days of prisons and electronic tagging, people needed to know who criminals were. For that reason, after sentencing, the guilty person would be mutilated in some way to make them more readily identifiable. This started with things like ears being chopped off, hands being severed, testicles being removed, and eyeballs plucked out. Over time, it was considered preferable to brand people.

King Edward VI passed a law in 1547 which required that all vagabonds, Gypsies and beggars be branded with the letter 'V' on their breast. Brawlers (those engaged in noisy fights and quarrels) were to be branded with the letter 'F' for 'Fraymaker'. Slaves who ran away from their masters were branded with the letter 'S' on their cheek or forehead.

From the reign of King Henry VII (1485-1509), branding was used for offences where the guilty person claimed 'benefit of clergy' as a defence or for those found guilty of manslaughter. They would be branded on the thumb. This ensured that they could only use benefit of clergy as a defence no more than once.

PUNISHMENT & TORTURE 203

From 1698 onwards, those convicted of petty theft or larceny and who claimed benefit of clergy in their defence were "*burnt in the most visible part of the left cheek, nearest the nose.*" This caused a problem with unemployment. No-one wanted to employ a branded convict. As a result, this law was repealed in 1707.

In the 18th century, those found guilty of counterfeiting, were likely to find themselves being branded on their right cheek with the letter 'R' for 'rogue'.

It wasn't just thieves, murderers, Gypsies and vagabonds that were branded. Those found guilty of uttering blasphemous words suffered branding, as did those constantly in a state of drunkenness. Blasphemers had their tongues branded. Branding could also be applied to the forehead, the cheek, the hands or the arms.

The branding iron used was usually a long iron bolt with a wooden handle which the brander would hold. On the opposite end of the iron bolt would be a raised letter. There were different branding irons containing other letters for the various types of offence. One such iron has been preserved in the dock at the Crown Court in Lancaster Castle. It carries the letter 'M' denoting the accused was a 'malefactor' (a wrong-doer). In a typical courtroom setup, there are two iron loops next to the branding iron, which held the prisoner's hand in place during the branding. After applying the brand, the brander would turn to the judge and say, "*A fair mark, my lord.*"

For most prisoners, branding was finally abolished in 1829.

Some of the standard branding marks used were:

B - Blasphemy

D - Drunkenness

D - Deserter

F - Fraymaker or Felon

M - Manslaughter or Murderer

M - Malefactor

P - Perjurer

R - Rogue

S - Slave

SL - Seditious Libeller

SS - Slave stealer

SS - Sower of sedition

T - Thief

King Canute's Punishment For Crimes Worse Than Theft

King Canute (1016-1035) issued his second law, which was remarkably specific, if not horrendously painful, for a 'greater crime' than theft. The punishment was the removal of the offender's eyes, nose, ears, upper lip and scalp. The punishment was for the removal of all of those body parts.

Punishment For Thieving Slaves

During the reign of King Edmund (921-946), the master-servant relationship was going very strong in England. A servant stealing from his master was considered a highly sinful act. Later, laws would regard this as an act of petty treason.

However, King Edmund's third law details the punishment for light-fingered slaves. It lists scourging (whipping with great suffering), removing the scalp and mutilating the little finger as punishment. The sentence was to suffer all three of those together.

Public Stocks Are Still Legal

Public stocks have been a common sight in England since the mid-fourteenth century. It was a place of public humiliation and a strong deterrent for repeat offenders. Passers-by could pelt those locked up in the stocks with anything from rotten fruit and vegetables, old shoes, stones and blocks of wood, and even raw sewage. It's not hard to see that public stocks were seen as an undesirable method of punishment by many offenders.

In 1351, King Edward III passed a law which stated that anyone demanding or offering higher wages would be placed in the village stocks for up to 3 days. This law was amended in 1405 by King Henry IV. It now required *"every town and village to maintain a set of stocks in which to punish vagabonds, layabouts and drunkards."*

In 1494, a law was introduced to punish lazy workers. It stated, *"Vagabonds, idle and suspected persons shall be set in the stocks for three days and three nights and have none other sustenance but bread and water and then shall be put out of Town."* Repeat offenders were set in the stocks for six days and six nights.

Public stocks have never been formally abolished in law. They were used regularly up until the 1870s, for various offences. Records show the last use of the public stocks for punishment occurred in Newbury in 1872. This was the case of Mark Tuck, a local rag and bone merchant and known alcoholic. He had already served time in Reading gaol, but this had not discouraged his drinking. On a Monday evening, he was found guilty of drunk and disorderly behaviour in the parish church. The Newbury stocks had not been used for 26 years, so when Tuck was sentenced to be set in the stocks, it caused a local sensation, and hundreds of people came to watch. Tuck was seated on a stool. His legs were secured in the stocks just after 1pm. The church clock would chime each quarter of the hour, causing the crowds to jeer Tuck. He was eventually released four hours later. This was the last recorded time that public stocks were used anywhere in the UK.

Interestingly, while the public pillory had been banned in 1837, the public stocks remain legal to this day. However, their use would undoubtedly breach the Human Rights Act (1998).

The Public Pillory

The pillory was a place of public entertainment where the townsfolk would crowd to see who was locked in each week for humiliation. The crowds would often taunt, laugh and jeer the offenders. This was all part of the punishment. Typically, the public would also throw rotten vegetables, offal, stones, eggs, mud, animal faeces and sometimes even dead animals at the offender locked in the pillory. On occasions, the crowds would become so rowdy they would throw bricks and large stones, causing serious injury and sometimes death to those locked in the pillory.

The pillory consisted of a wooden block, hinged to lift up, whilst the offender placed their head and hands through the holes provided. The top wooden block would then be lowered down and secured with a lock. As an instrument of humiliation, they were mainly placed at locations that attracted the most spectators, for example, in market squares and at crossroads. They were often erected on raised platforms so they could be seen from a long distance away. Some pillories also had a board next to them upon which the offender's crimes would be written for all to see.

The offender would be forced to bend down with their head and hands stuck through the pillory. Due to the length of time that many offenders were forced to stand in the pillory, this became an exhausting position, over time becoming extremely uncomfortable. Often humiliation wasn't enough, and sentencing would include the further punishment of having their head shaved, whipped, branded on the cheek or forehead or having their ears nailed to the pillory. There have been occasions when the ear was cut off altogether, leaving it nailed to the pillory block.

A famous occupant of the public pillory was the priest Titus Oates. He was arrested for involvement in the 1678 Catholic plot to murder King Charles II. He was charged with sedition, imprisoned and sentenced to a (very hefty) fine of £100,000. When King James II acceded to the throne in 1685, he had Oates retried for perjury. This time, Oates was sentenced to life imprisonment, with occasional displays in the public pillory. He was taken to his cell and forced to wear a hat, upon which was written *"Titus Oates, convicted upon full evidence of two horrid perjuries."* Following this, he was put on display in the pillory at the gate of Westminster Hall, where he was pelted with eggs from gathered crowds. On this first day of punishment, the crowds became very rowdy and threw sharp objects at him. Some hit him on the head, drawing blood. It is said that he nearly lost his life in the public pillory on this day. The next day he was locked in a pillory in London, and on the third day, he was stripped, tied to a cart and publicly whipped through the streets from Aldgate to Newgate. On the fourth day, he underwent the same ordeal, being dragged from Newgate to Tyburn, all the while being publicly whipped with crowds throwing objects at him. This wasn't the last Oates would see of the pillory. According to his sentence, he was required to spend five days of each year for the rest of his life in the following public pillories:

- 24th of April: the pillory at Tyburn
- 9th of August: the pillory in front of the gate of Westminster Hall
- 10th of August: the pillory at Charing Cross
- 11th of August: the pillory at Temple
- 2nd of September: the pillory at the Royal Exchange

Fortunately for Oates, he only spent three years in prison. In 1689, with the accession to the throne of King William & Queen Mary, he was given a pardon.

The last person to be sentenced to spending time in the pillory was Peter James Bossy. He was found guilty of *"wilful and corrupt perjury."* At his trial, he was sentenced to be imprisoned for six months in Newgate Prison, followed by seven years penal transportation to Australia. As part of his sentence, he also had to spend one hour in the public pillory in London. This took place on 22nd June 1830.

The pillory was formally abolished in England and Wales on 30th June 1837.

Whipping

From the mediaeval period, whipping has been a standard method of punishment for minor crimes. Whipping became so prevalent as a punishment in prisons that wooden apparatus, the 'birching donkey', was provided to accommodate the whipping. The offender would either be forced to lean over the device to receive their punishment, or they would be whipped, standing against it in an upright position.

Whipping as a form of punishment against women was made illegal in 1820.

In a curious case from the Isle of Man in 1972, Anthony Tyrer, a 15-year-old boy, was administered three strokes of the birch. This was after he had assaulted a schoolmate. His birching was conducted at the local police station, by a policeman, in the presence of Tyrer's father and a doctor. To carry out his sentence, Tyrer was forced to take down his trousers and underpants and bend over a table in front of the onlookers for the punishment to be administered. His lawyers claimed this caused him undue anxiety and suffering. The matter was challenged legally, going all the way to the European Court of Human Rights in 1978. The judges had to decide whether Tyrer's birching constituted degrading treatment contrary to the European Convention on Human Rights.

Scavenger's Daughter

The Scavenger's Daughter was a torture device that seems to have been lovingly named after the inventor's daughter. The device, also known as Skeffington's Irons, was named after its inventor, Sir. William Skevington. He was the Lieutenant of the Tower of London during the reign of King Henry VIII, a notorious period of State torture in British history. Skevington must have seen the sheer power of The Rack and its ability to extract information from prisoners about their co-conspirators. The idea behind The Rack is to stretch a prisoner to confession. Skevington must have wondered what it would be like to do the opposite and instead compress a prisoner.

It was an A-frame-shaped metal device. The head was strapped into one end of the device (the top point of the A-frame), the hands shackled into the midpoint, and the legs spread out at the ends. The head was forced into a downward position, and the knees were forced into an upright sitting position. This stress position was highly uncomfortable for the prisoner over periods of long-time. Some variations of this device contained a hinge in the middle, which the torturer could screw to tighten the hinge. This crushed the prisoner further and further into a ball. Over time, the compression would become so great that blood would gush from the prisoner's face and fingertips. The spine would become so misaligned, and the ribs could snap.

A Scavenger's Daughter is currently on display in the Tower of London. Although it is only briefly mentioned in some of the Tower documents, we know that it was mainly used for prisoners accused of high treason against Queen Elizabeth I.

The Rack

The rack is probably the most famous of all torture instruments used in the UK. It was designed to stretch the victim slowly until their limbs became dislocated, eventually tearing them from their sockets. This caused such fear in the prisoners that the mere sight of the rack would often immediately extract a confession. It was common practice for prisoners to be forced to watch other people being tortured on the rack.

The rack consisted of a raised rectangular wooden frame. Some racks would have a roller at one end, whilst others had a roller at both ends. The legs would be attached to a movable bar at one end, whilst the prisoner's wrists would be tied firmly to the other end of the wooden frame or another movable bar. The torturer slowly turned the handle attached to the top roller as the interrogation progressed. This increased the tension on the prisoner's chains and, right from the outset, caused unbearable pain. The procedure continued with the torturer turning the handle which rotated the rollers, slowly dislocating the prisoner's joints.

The rack was intended to produce extreme pain through torture. It certainly achieved its aim! Most of the time, the victim's bones would be dislocated from the joints resulting in a loud popping sound caused by torn ligaments and cartilage. If the torturer continued to turn the handles, the prisoner's limbs would be torn off, rendering the arms and legs useless. Prisoners knew the result would be suffering with permanent disability for life, which was often enough to shock them into confession or providing names of co-conspirators.

Later variations of the rack included the addition of spikes which penetrated the victims' backs whilst their limbs were pulled from their joints. Some executioners preferred to tie the prisoner face down, resulting in the spiked rotating drum piercing their abdomen and disembowelling them simultaneously.

Thumb Screws

This device, whilst not as lethal as other torture methods, must leave you in no doubt that the pain suffered by those on the receiving end of the torture must have been accompanied by moments of wishing their death came swifter. The device itself was very similar to a vice. The prisoner's thumbs would be placed between two metal plates. A large screw sat on top of the device. The torturer would turn the screw, pushing the top metal plate downwards, painfully crushing the thumbs between the metal plates. There were different variations of this device. Some included protruding studs inside the metal plates, which bored down into the prisoners' thumbs to inflict a greater pain.

These devices were also applied to crush prisoners' big toes. Larger devices of the same design were used for crushing prisoners' knees, elbows and wrists.

Tarring and Feathering

We often associate the punishment of tarring and feathering with acts of humiliation committed during religious and racial persecutions. These have sadly been all too evident as recently as the twentieth century. It emerged in England during the early mediaeval period as a form of physical punishment used to enforce local justice.

Typically, the accused would have been stripped to the waist. Often their hair would have been shaved. Hot tar was poured or ladled onto the accused, causing unbearable pain. Following this, he would then have feathers thrown on him or be forcibly rolled around on a bed of feathers which stuck to the sticky tar. There are reports that on some occasions, the feathers were also set alight to inflict further suffering. As a final act of humiliation, the accused would then be paraded around the local town on the back of a cart for all to see. Often, the sheer humiliation would force the accused to leave the town altogether.

Hard Labour

Victorian prisons were known to be harsh. As if prison life wasn't hard enough, many prisoners were also sentenced to hard labour.

A law from 1865 required that all males aged 16 or over sentenced to imprisonment with hard labour had to spend at least three months of their sentence in what was known as Labour Order. After three months, the level of hard labour could reduce in severity.

In 1877, these three months of severe hard labour were reduced to just one month. Hard labour was banned on Sundays, Christmas Day, Good Friday or days appointed for public fasts or thanksgivings.

Since its introduction, several forms of hard labour have been used in prison. Some forms of hard labour have a practical purpose that benefits society or some trade. For example, oakum picking, basket weaving, mat-making, net-making and blacksmithing. Whereas other forms are just purely punishing and used as a deterrent, like the crank, the treadmill or shot drill. Shot drill required prisoners to lean forward without bending their knees and lift heavy objects like a cannonball or block of stone to chest height. They would then move three paces to the right, place it back on the ground and step back three paces. This repetitive cycle would see the prisoner moving a pile of heavy objects from one pile on the left to another on the right and back again.

Picking Oakum was another common form of hard labour in prisons. They would be provided lengths of old rope and required to untwist each strand from the rope, separating them into their individual strands. It had a practical use because the rope could be reused. Unfortunately, the ropes were often covered in tar and picking them apart led to finger blisters and bleeding. The well-known writer Oscar Wilde was one such prisoner required to pick oakum during his stay.

Another prisoner was 15-year-old William Anderson from Lancashire, convicted at the Manchester Petty Sessions for stealing brass fittings from a deserted house. He was sentenced to three months imprisonment with hard labour.

Any form of imprisonment with hard labour was abolished in 1948.

The Crank

The crank machine was a much-hated Victorian punishment, commonly known as 'The Crank'. A prisoner was forced to turn a crank by hand on the side of this machine. When turned, the crank moved four large paddles through sand or gravel enclosed in a drum. This made it harder to turn the crank. Prisoners sentenced to hard labour often found themselves forced to use the crank machine. Those who chose to misbehave in prison also found themselves forced to turn the crank. It was both boring and exhausting work. The prisoner was required to turn the heavy metal crank handle anywhere between 6,000 and 14,400 times in a six-hour period. To make the task harder, a prison warder could adjust the tightening screw on the side of the crank machine. This made the task either easier or harder, depending on the level of punishment the prisoner was owed and how much the prison warder disliked them. This is where the term '*screw*' originates when referring to prison officers.

The crank was abolished in 1898.

Treadmills

The prison treadmill very quickly came to be hated as the worst of all the forms of punishment and hard labour. Also known as treadwheels, they were first introduced into British prisons in 1818. The purpose of the treadmill was to be exhausting labour and a mind-numbing task. It was boring and repetitive. Prisoners were not allowed to talk to each other.

The treadmills were long wooden cylinders with metal frames, each containing 24 steps, looking very similar to large paddle wheels. On the outside of the treadmills were wooden steps. Each of these treadmills was able to accommodate between 18 and 25 prisoners at any one time. The large wheels turned under the power of the prisoners walking upon its steps. This forced prisoners to move their weight on to the next step above continually. It was like a never-ending staircase. Between each prisoner was a wooden partition. So, the prisoners had to climb this long staircase for hours, unable to see or talk to anyone else. All they could do was stare at the wall in front of them. They had to walk for six hours a day, following a quick-change shift pattern of 15 minutes of walking followed by five minutes break. Each prisoner would be forced to walk up to 18,000 feet per day.

In June 1888, 20-year-old Arthur Simmonds received a sentence of 18 months with hard labour at Pentonville prison. His offence was stealing a letter. After serving just three days on the prison treadmill, he could barely walk and was unable to eat food. He was taken to the prison infirmary and died a few days later.

Treadmills were finally abolished in British prisons in 1898.

Riding The Whirligig

Whilst this torture contraption was solely confined to those in the military, it's too fun not to give it a brief mention in this book.

Before you continue reading, let me ask you to consider whether you have ever been on one of those fairground rides, like the Waltzer, that spins around, where you experience varying levels of g-force, and feel like you're being pushed to the back of your seat? This is essentially what this punishment method is, except you can't just stop the ride and get off after a couple of minutes.

The Whirligig was a six-foot high cylindrical wooden cage suspended in the air, connected through pivots to a post on the ground. The prisoner would be forced inside the cage, after which the central post would spin, turning the cage at very high speeds.

Riders could not help but feel nauseous, repeatedly vomiting and often resulting in injuries like dislocated bones, torn muscles and even unconsciousness.

This device created such a spectacle that other soldiers crowded around to watch. The purpose of this device was purely to humiliate the unfortunate 'rider' and deter them from their wayward behaviour.

Chapter Seventeen

Religion & Puritanical Behaviour

Those dastardly Puritans are at it again in this chapter, with Christmas featuring heavily. It seems Christmas was banned. It wasn't an outright ban, but no-one was permitted to celebrate Christmas or any other festive period during their Puritan rule. There was to be no singing of Christmas carols, no festive family get-togethers with large meals ... even putting up decorations could land you in the village stocks.

In this chapter, we look at just how grim Christmas Day can get, especially if you have some Puritans staying as your guests.

The torment doesn't end when you die. You may be summoned to court four centuries later ... it happens!

Christmas is Banned!

Following the Civil War and the killing of King Charles I, the Puritan Parliament set about dismantling many of the freedoms they claimed to be fighting to keep. They introduced a law that effectively banned Christmas altogether. On 8th June 1647, they passed a law banning all festivals and holy days, including Christmas, Easter and Whitsuntide. They felt that Christmas had become too rowdy.

This law made it a criminal offence to celebrate the feast of Christmas. There was to be no getting together with family members over Christmas lunch. Shops were forced to remain open on Christmas Day. Any Christmas or Easter decorations were banned. There was to be absolutely no partying or lavish eating. Those holy days were meant to be replaced with a day of fasting. To enforce this, Puritan soldiers patrolled the streets of London and other major cities, confiscating decorations and anything that looked like party food. On Christmas Eve, Town Criers were brought out onto the streets in force, ringing their bells and shouting *"No Christmas! No Christmas!"* as a reminder. People were not allowed to attend church on Christmas Day.

It will come as no surprise that the public didn't take too kindly to this law, and it wasn't long before riots, and general disorder broke out. On Christmas Day in 1647, a mass protest broke out around the water fountain in Cornhill, London. Angry revellers draped holly, ivy, and other Christmas decorations around the water fountain. They prevented the Mayor of London and his officials from removing these Christmas decorations. Constables were called and started to arrest the partygoers. The result was violence, utter mayhem and the death of one of the partygoers in Newgate Prison.

Riots broke out elsewhere in England too. In Ipswich, a protester was killed on Christmas Day. Ironically his name was 'Christmas'. In Canterbury, large crowds assembled to demand a Christmas Day sermon. The authorities intervened and took a heavy-handed approach to break up the congregation. One congregation member assaulted a soldier, which triggered an ensuing riot, spilling out onto the streets. They trashed the mayor's house, attacked the shops that had been ordered to remain open on Christmas Day and took control of Canterbury. They held the city for the whole Christmas period, during which they decorated doorways with holly and continued their Christmas festivities unhindered. Meanwhile, at St. Margaret's Church in Westminster, the minister Nicholas Bernard had been arrested and thrown into Fleet Street prison for attempting to preach a sermon on Christmas Day. There were other reports in the newspapers of churchgoers attending Christmas Day services armed with weapons and guarding the church doors with swords whilst the minister was in his pulpit.

You Must Fast on Christmas Day

On 24th August 1642, the Puritan Parliament passed a law ordering that the last Wednesday of every month is set aside as a day of fasting. The public were not happy with this. They were even more unhappy when in 1644, this mandated day of fasting fell on Christmas Day itself. The majority wanted to celebrate Christmas, whereas the law required that day to be set aside for fasting.

A request was made to Parliament to waive this law just for that year to enable people to celebrate Christmas with their families, enjoying the festive frolics. As we know, the Puritans disliked festivities. As expected, Parliament refused. Instead, they published a public notice. The notice spelt out that the day would be spent fasting. It reminded people that they had forgotten the memory of Christ. Just in case anyone decided not to take this public notice seriously, on 19th December 1644, they passed a further law. These laws were repealed the instant King Charles II was restored to the throne in May 1660.

Singing Christmas Carols Could Get You in Trouble

It is well-known that Puritans disliked the celebration of Christmas. They saw any Christmas festivities, including the singing of Christmas carols, as sinful acts. Christmas festivities were banned by law in 1644. Three years later, Parliament abolished the feast of Christmas altogether. While singing was not itself banned, Oliver Cromwell and the Puritans sought to ban any excesses or elaborate music being played in church. They did permit the singing of psalms in church. However, the singing of Christmas carols represented an act of celebration and the festivities of Christmas, which were all banned.

It's Perfectly Legal to Drive Around With a Corpse in Your Car

According to the law, the body of a baby, child or adult may be moved anywhere within England and Wales without using a coffin or without any permission, as long as the Coroner's work is not obstructed. It is a myth that a fee or toll would have to be paid when conveying a dead body across boundaries, from county to county. This is not true. The only exemption is that a coroner must first consent before a dead body can be taken out of England and Wales.

Bizarrely, there aren't many laws covering the transport of dead bodies, whether animal or human. You don't even need to place a body into a coffin. There are also no set time limits regarding the disposal of the dead. So, you literally can drive around the streets for weeks with the corpse of Aunty Ivy strapped to your roof rack or thrown into the boot of a car. However, I suspect the local Constabulary may regularly pull you over.

Thomas Becket Was Summoned to Court Four Centuries After His Death

Thomas Becket was once one of the most influential figures in England. After serving as the Lord Chancellor in 1162, he became the Archbishop of Canterbury. However, his views differed from those of his King, Henry II, over the power, rights and privileges enjoyed by the Church. This created a power struggle between Church and State that continued for centuries. On 29th December 1170, Becket was killed by four knights who believed they were carrying out the instructions of the King. Immediately, Becket was seen as a hero. On 21st February 1173, he was made 'Saint Thomas of Canterbury' by Pope Alexander III.

On 7th July 1220, Becket's remains were moved from his first tomb to a recently built shrine in Trinity Chapel. The event was attended by the Archbishop of Canterbury, many noblemen and, most notably, King Henry III. Over the next three centuries, the remains and relics in St Thomas' shrine were visited by many on pilgrimages, including King Henry VIII and his first wife, Katherine of Aragon. However, things changed when he took a shine to lady-in-waiting Anne Boleyn and decided to ask Pope Clement VII to cancel his marriage. The Pope refused. The King decided to reject Catholicism and create the Church of England, appointing himself as the Supreme Head of the Church. He ordered the Catholic Monasteries to close. Then labelled Saint Thomas Becket as a traitor, summoning him to appear before the Star Chamber to answer for his crimes of treason against the King's ancestor. In an attempt to wipe Becket from the history books, on 5th September 1538, the King and his soldiers arrived in Canterbury, where they removed the gold and precious jewels after dismantling Becket's shrine. He then had Becket's bones burned and scattered to the winds and proclaimed that he was to be un-sainted.

Marriage on The Cheap

Things seem to get particularly colourful during the seventeenth century. One particular group became a real problem for the churches around that time. These were known as *Patricios* or Stroller priests. For those who wished to get married, the churches would often first check whether they were able to read a passage from the Bible. If not, the church could refuse to marry them. This created a situation where people who couldn't read or those from the poor and lower classes could not be officially married by the church. There were also occasions when a happy couple who didn't fit into those categories, did not receive their parents' blessings. They, too, would be refused an official marriage in church. These people, desperately in love and probably more deserving of an official marriage than some unscrupulous sorts who would have just thrown money at the church, would often turn to the Stroller priests to officiate their wedding. These were men who travelled around the countryside performing fake marriage ceremonies. The marriage union was not recognised by the church or by law. However, many couples felt that it at least cemented their union in the eyes of God. Like the church, Stroller priests would require payment before undertaking this 'marriage ceremony', but the fee was nowhere near the church's expected donation.

Perhaps the most peculiar aspect of this marriage ceremony conducted by Stroller priests was that the happy couple would be married whilst standing over a bed of leaves. If that wasn't absurd enough, underneath the leaves was the corpse of a dead horse. The ceremony would be concluded when the newly designated husband and wife shook hands over the dead horse.

People of Jewish Faith Banned From Living in Conwy

Conwy is a walled market town in North Wales, standing alongside the west bank of the River Conwy. I spent many summers here during the formative years of my upbringing. Conwy derives its name from the old Welsh words *cyn* (chief) and *gwy* (water). The River Conwy was originally called 'Cynwy'.

The famous Conwy Castle and its town walls were ordered to be built by King Edward I during his conquest of Wales. However, this isn't the only thing King Edward was known for in Conwy. Upon granting its Charter, he ordered that no "*Jews*" and no "*Welsh*" were permitted to live within his town walls of Conwy.

This issue was raised in Parliament as recently as 20th February 2019.

People of Jewish Faith Banned From England

Persecution of the Jews began almost as soon as Jewish communities arrived in England following the Norman conquest of 1066. It became progressively worse throughout the thirteenth century. At the time, Jews were considered property of the Crown, having Royal protection against antisemitism.

Two years after coming to the throne, in 1218, King Henry III passed a law, which made England the first country to require Jews to wear a special badge to identify them. Taxes levied on the Jews rose to intense levels. In 1222, the Archbishop of Canterbury passed a set of laws restricting the rights of Jews to engage with Christians in England. They were also banned from building new synagogues or owning slaves. In 1253, Henry III passed a law, increasing segregation and once again requiring Jewish people to wear a yellow badge to identify them.

King Edward I passed a law in 1275. This placed even more restrictions on Jews in England, most notably an almost outright ban on them providing money loans. This law also released anyone who currently owed any money to Jews. Any Jew above the age of seven had to wear a yellow badge made from felt. All Jews aged 12 and above had to pay an annual tax of 3p.

In the 15 years since the passing of that law, King Edward I realised that many Jews were still practising as money lenders. Consequently, on 18th July 1290, he passed a new law, which formally expelled all Jews from the Kingdom of England. He notified all his sheriffs that every Jew would be expelled no later than All Saints' Day, which fell on 1st November that year. This edict remained in force for over 360 years before Oliver Cromwell put a stop to it in 1656.

Claiming 'Benefit of Clergy'

Since the Middle Ages, for all but the most serious offences, a useful method for being spared the death penalty was to claim the 'Benefit of clergy'. This was an ancient right afforded to the Church, which allowed it to punish its members according to religious law.

When an offender claimed the benefit of clergy, they would be handed over to the Church to be dealt with by them and not the local authorities. It became impossible to know who was a genuine churchgoer, so several methods were devised to determine this. One such method was to get the offender to read a passage from the Bible, usually verses from the 51st Psalm. This became known as the 'neck verse'. It was an unfair test, considering the majority of the population of England at the time were unable to read. Generally, only scholars, noblemen and the clergy could read and write. So, it was at the judge's discretion regarding the choice of text to be read and whether they would go easy on the person being tested. The benefit of clergy was initially only offered to men. By 1623, women were permitted to claim the benefit of clergy for theft where the stolen items were less than 10 shillings in value. By 1691, women were granted this right on equal terms with men.

Benefit of clergy was finally abolished during the reign of King George IV, on 21st June 1827.

Claiming 'Right of Sanctuary'

Since Anglo-Saxon times, fugitives have escaped the death penalty and other serious punishments by claiming the right of sanctuary in a church. The only problem was that immediately following their sanctuary; they would have to permanently leave England if they hadn't resolved the issue from which they were running.

In 693AD, Ine, King of the West Saxons, passed a law stating that anyone accused of an offence carrying the death penalty, could flee to the church, and his life would be spared. In 887AD, Alfred the Great, King of the West Saxons, announced that it was law for anyone to flee to the church and remain there in the privilege of sanctuary for three nights. If anyone hurt or wounded that person whilst in the sanctuary of the church, they were themselves forced to suffer the same full penalty of the person claiming sanctuary, along with an additional 120 shillings to the ministers of that church. This later changed to sanctuary lasting seven days.

Following the Norman conquest, in 1070, William the Conqueror declared that the privilege of sanctuary was only temporary and would last for 40 days.

In the centre of the sanctuary was a *'fridstool'* (chair of peace). The church sanctuary usually extended in a one-mile radius from the fridstool. Although, sometimes, it could just be confined to the boundary walls of the church. Once a person had claimed sanctuary, they could not be dragged out of the church or in any way harmed. They were not permitted to take potshots at their adversaries through the church windows.

After 40 days, if the offender had been unable to resolve the issue, he would have to leave the country. He would have to make his way to the nearest sailing port and take passage on the first ship to sail out of the country. If no ship were leaving, he would have to return each day, wading into the sea until it reached his knees before turning back to the shore. He would have to continue this unusual practice each day, irrespective of any harsh weather, until a ship was available to take him out of the country. If at any point he failed, even just by not turning up one day, perhaps because he was ill, the law immediately took over. As he had already confessed to his crime, he would most likely be executed.

In 1530, King Henry VIII abolished the right of sanctuary for those accused of treason against the Crown. From then on, those who claimed sanctuary had to remain in the church for the rest of their life, wearing a badge 20 inches long and forbidden from leaving during daylight hours.

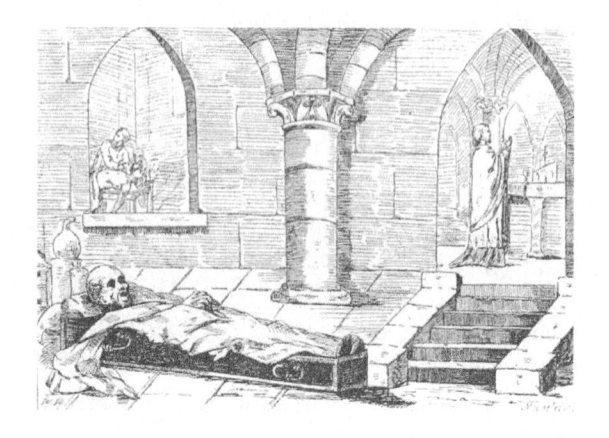

Illegal to Not Attend Church on Sundays

The second law that Queen Elizabeth I passed during her reign was The Act of Uniformity (1558). It ordered that every person inhabiting the realm must, unless they have a lawful or reasonable excuse, attend and *"report to their Parish Church or Chapel"*, every Sunday and any other days ordained as Holy Days and whilst there, to abide by the Common Prayer and Preaching. The punishment for failing to attend church was *"pain of punishment by the censures of the church"* and to forfeit 12 pence for each offence of non-attendance.

In 1580, the Queen passed another law that increased the previous penalty for non-attendance at church. It required anyone over 16 years to attend church, chapel, or their usual place of common prayer. If they failed to do so for up to a month, they were fined £20. If they continued failing to attend church, imprisonment was the likely outcome.

Chapter Eighteen
ROADS, PATHWAYS & WATERWAYS

Over the centuries, many laws have been passed to ensure communities can live together peacefully and to maintain both public safety and hygiene.

From the mischievous child playing knock and run along his street to the unsuspecting apple scrumper who receives the death penalty for damaging a tree, one thing is for sure, a great many of us will be breaking these laws regularly.

In this chapter, we look at some of the laws and regulations surrounding our everyday use of the Great British roads, pathways and even our waterways. We also examine some of the harsher punishments handed out to those unlucky few who dared to break the law.

Knock And Run

Knock, Down, Ginger ... Ding, Dong, Ditch ... or as we call it in the UK, Knock and Run.

Even in the UK, this game has different regional names. In the North East, it's known as 'Knocky Nine Doors'. Elsewhere it's 'Knock Down Ginger', 'Chickenelly', 'Knock a Door Run' and even, somewhat menacingly, 'Knock granny out of bed'. It's a prank played mainly by children with origins dating back to the 19th century. Essentially, the knocker would knock on the victim's front door or ring their doorbell and run away before the door could be answered. As amusing as this can be for children, imagine if the victim is an elderly person or someone with severely restrictive mobility issues. Each time they get up to answer the door, they put themselves at risk.

What might seem to many to be a perfectly harmless yet annoying game is, in fact, a criminal offence outlawed in the UK in the mid-19th century. Fortunately, in today's world of camera doorbells and ever-present CCTV, knock and run no longer enjoys the popularity it once did because it's now a lot easier to identify the offender.

A specific offence was created in 1854 to put a stop to this in London. It made it an offence for *"Every person who shall wilfully and wantonly disturb any inhabitant by pulling or ringing any doorbell or knocking at any door without lawful excuse, or who shall wilfully and unlawfully extinguish the light of any lamp."* This offence was created in the days of gas-powered street lamps.

A few years earlier, in 1847, Knock and Run had already become an offence nationally.

This law was introduced to prevent people from causing annoyance or disturbance to others. The 1847 law was repealed in 2015, but Knock and Run still remains an offence in London. That said, it would no doubt be covered by other laws that deal with disorderly conduct.

Illegal to Carry a Plank of Wood or Ladder Down The Street

This has nothing to do with the recent craze of 'planking'. Although, that certainly should have been an offence ... against sanity. By now, many people will have heard the myth about it being illegal to carry a plank of wood along a street. It isn't a myth. There actually is a law from 1839 that makes carrying a plank of wood an offence, which risks a heavy fine. This particular law was introduced to keep pavements and pathways free from obstruction and prevents anyone from blocking the pavements with cumbersome or oversized objects. It is still an offence now to obstruct the pavement making it necessary for pedestrians to have to walk on the road. This is understandable because it introduces pedestrians to the additional unnecessary risk of passing traffic.

Until 2015, this was also an offence across the whole of the UK. It now just remains an offence in London.

Flying a Kite in the Street is Illegal

In Victorian England, much of the fun was restricted to designated areas like public parks. The government was keen to limit people playing in the streets where they could pose a danger to each other.

A law passed in London in 1839 made it an offence to fly a kite in a public place if it caused *"annoyance to other people."*

Under a law passed in 1847, flying a kite became an offence everywhere in the UK and not just in London. Incidentally, the same law would also prohibit playing Pokémon Go or even a humble game of chess if it causes annoyance to any passers-by.

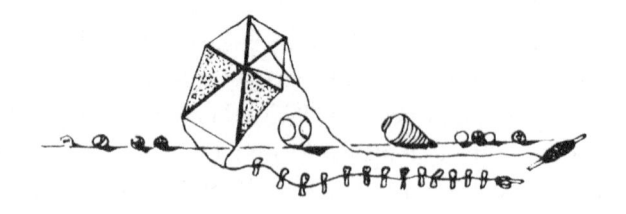

The highest you are permitted to fly a kite is 4,879.54 metres. However, I can't think of a situation where this would occur. A kite can not be flown at a height of more than 60 metres above ground level. Technically, kites are classed as aircraft and, therefore, subject to some additional regulations. You must not fly your kite more than 30 metres (100 feet) above ground level within 5 kilometres (3 miles) of an airfield. You should also avoid flying kites along take-off and landing flight paths. If you insist on flying your kite at night, it must be fitted with lights.

Illegal to Erect Your Washing Line in the Street

Things like washing lines, fluttering towels and underwear can be remarkably unsightly, especially if there's a washing line outside multiple dwellings on the same street.

A law passed in 1847 made it an offence for "*Every Person who places any Line, Cord, or Pole across any Street, or hangs or places any Clothes thereon.*" This offence is punishable by a fine of up to £1,000.

This law was only repealed as recently as 2015. Sadly, for those living in London, an earlier law from 1839 still exists and would make it an offence if you hung your washing line from a window or building, if it annoyed others in the street. However, hanging it from a fence seems to be no offence.

Death for Damaging Trees

We might today feel that the law can sometimes be pretty harsh and restrictive on our rights, but that's nothing compared to how it used to be. I'm not talking about Norman or early Anglo-Saxon law but a relatively recent piece of legislation passed in 1722 during the reign of King George I.

I am referring to the infamous Black Act, otherwise known as the 'Bloody Code', because it introduced the death penalty for over 350 criminal offences. You literally would be hanged for things like damaging an orchard or a garden or in any way destroying trees. Anyone caught conspiring with others to damage trees or rescue anyone who had been imprisoned for such an offence would receive the same death sentence.

Illegal to Damage Grass

In Britain, we love our grass so much that we decided to also create laws to protect it. A law passed in 1857 made it a criminal offence to do anything that wilfully damages a village green or interrupts its use as a place for exercise and recreation.

A further law was passed in 1876 to reinforce the importance of preserving our village greens. It made it an offence to interfere with or disturb a town or village green. This law was passed not so much to protect the grass but rather to prevent disruption to activities that might be played upon the grass. These are such things as community games like cricket or bowling. Both laws are still live on the statute books.

In September 2022, a man was fined and faced court costs amounting to £400 after riding his quadbike and damaging grass in Winsford Park, Cheshire. So, if you're a visitor to the UK, please remember not to injure our grass or disrupt our public exercise and recreation. We might get a little upset.

The Orchestral Manoeuvres of an Ice Cream Van

Laws were passed to reduce the annoyance of ice cream van chimes. The Control of Pollution Act (1974) makes it an offence to operate or permit the operation of any loudspeaker of the 'ice-cream van chimes' type in the street outside the hours of 12 noon and 7 pm on the same day. The loudspeaker on ice cream vans may also not be operated in a way that annoys people in the vicinity. In addition, the chimes must not be sounded for more than 12 seconds at a time or more often than once every 2 minutes. They must also not be sounded more often than once every two hours in the same length of the street. Ice cream van chimes must not be sounded within 50 metres of a school (during school hours), hospitals and places of worship (on Sundays and other recognised days of worship).

Driving Cattle Through the Streets

The title may, at first, seem a little misleading. That's because it's not a term we often use these days. In the Victorian age, cars weren't even a thing on the road. Occasionally you might have found a locomotive driving on the road or a horse and cart. The term 'driving cattle' refers to moving a herd of cattle from one place to another. This could be a farmer driving his cattle from his field to the local market.

A law passed in 1867 prohibited anyone from walking his cows through the street between 10am and 7pm. It does, however, provide an exemption if you first obtain the permission of the Commissioner of the Metropolitan Police. Any person found guilty of this offence is liable to a penalty not exceeding ten shillings for each head of cattle.

This offence only covers the London area. However, the rest of the country doesn't get away with it, either. The Highway Act (1980) made it an offence to allow horses, cattle, sheep, goats or swine to stray on or at the roadside.

Both of these laws are still active.

Bizarre Bylaws

Bylaws are laws created by local authorities. Over the centuries, local authorities have passed some incredible bylaws that would leave you howling for hours. The majority have since been repealed, although occasionally, you can still come across some great examples from more recent times.

The County Borough of Blackburn felt it necessary to pass the following bylaw in 1933, which states, "*No person shall sound or play upon any musical or noisy instrument or sing in any street or public place within 100 yards of any place of public worship ... in which persons are for the time being assembled, to the annoyance or disturbance of any person.*" So, this rules out busking or playing your electric keyboard in the car park of the local church on Sunday mornings.

They also have a similar restriction on "*playing upon any musical or noisy instrument*" or even singing in the street within 100 yards of any hospital. Presumably, it would be perfectly acceptable to hum and whistle around hospitals. They passed a further bylaw to outlaw any 'wilful jostling' on the streets of Blackburn. It states that it is an offence if "*two or more persons assembled together wilfully obstruct the free use of any street, or wilfully jostle or annoy any foot passengers.*"

Not to be outdone, Congleton Borough Council in Cheshire felt it necessary to create a bylaw prohibiting indecent bathing. It states, "*no person shall within 200 yards of any street or public place, unless effectually screened from view, bathe from the bank or strand of any water, or from any boat thereon, without wearing a dress or covering sufficient to prevent indecent exposure of the person."*

Illegal to Slide on Ice or Snow in Any Street

Ice can be a genuine hazard for cars and people walking on the streets. In Victorian London, there seems to have been a craze of people sliding along the ice on terraced streets.

You can imagine the dangers involved, with passing horses and carts, perhaps even limited visibility from the river fog and people stepping out of their homes, only to be knocked off their feet by a passing ice skater. It became such a problem that they had to pass a law in 1839 to put a stop to it.

The rest of the UK was just fine. They could skate away. Until 1847, when a new law banned anyone from sliding upon ice or snow in the street. This was only repealed as recently as 2015. However, for those living in London, it is still an offence.

Illegal to Empty Your Toilet Between 6 AM & Midnight

Toilets, or '*the privy*' as it used to be called, weren't the same system we use today. No outflow or sewage pipe was running from the privy, and residents would have to carry their outdoor toilet to empty its contents into the nearby sewers.

These would often end up in the River Thames for residents of London.

With the increasing population in the 1800s, it soon became apparent that the number of toilets didn't match the population expansion. This resulted in up to a hundred people sharing the same toilet in inner-city areas of large cities like Manchester and London. Society started to realise that poor sanitary conditions led to increased disease, with raw sewage often finding its way back into the drinking water supply. This became ever more apparent during the cholera pandemic between 1826 and 1837, killing thousands of people. Lawmakers decided something had to be done about public sanitation and, more specifically, emptying sewage from the privy.

In 1839 a law was passed which meant that people were only allowed to empty their outdoor toilet between the hours of midnight and 6 o'clock in the morning.

This law was repealed in 1906.

Chapter Nineteen
THE ROYAL HOUSEHOLD

Centuries ago, the reigning Stuart kings regularly dissolved Parliament if they didn't agree with them. Eventually, Parliament had enough and chopped off The King's head. Fortunately, these days the Royal Family and Parliament have a smoother, more friendly relationship than they once did. In fact, things became perhaps a little too cosy with the Home Secretary having to be present to witness all Royal births. King Charles III was the first Royal baby to be born without this additional set of prying eyes.

Lazy soldiers better beware. Queen Victoria was certainly not amused when she came across some of her soldiers drunk and gambling. She ensured they would be punished ... for 100 years!

As you can imagine, this chapter dealing with the Royal household has had its fair share of myths over the years. You don't want to be hanged, drawn & quartered for affixing your postage stamps upside down.

Illegal to Stand Within 100 Yards of The Reigning Monarch Without Wearing Socks

A lot has been said about it being an offence to stand within 100 yards of the monarch whilst not wearing socks. Several monarchs over the centuries have passed laws to regulate clothing worn by various classes of people, including Kings Edward III and Henry VIII, as well as Queens Mary I and Elizabeth I. A law passed in May 1562 by Queen Elizabeth banned anyone from wearing shirts with *"outrageous double ruffs,"* or hose (trousers) of *"monstrous and outrageous greatness"* in the Royal court. These laws dealt with clothing and accessories, ruffs, hose and even overly-pointed shoes. There was, however, no such law, nor has there ever been, in relation to wearing socks within the Royal court. Most of these clothing laws were repealed during the reign of King James I.

All Beached Whales, Dolphins, Porpoises & Sturgeons Belong to The King

The *Prerogativa Regis* is an ancient law passed in 1322 by King Edward II. It stands for '*of the King's Prerogative*'. It states that *"the King shall have throughout the Realm, Whales and great Sturgeons taken in the Sea or elsewhere within the Realm."*

This means that King Charles now owns all whales, dolphins, porpoises and sturgeons taken from UK territorial waters or any that wash up onshore. All beached whales and sturgeons are classed as Royal fish and must be offered to the monarch. This now includes all dolphins and porpoises. It is said that the whale's head must be offered to The King and the tail offered to The Queen.

Indeed, this ancient law has never been repealed and popped up in 2004, when a sturgeon fish was caught in Swansea Bay and offered to the Royal household. Her Majesty The Queen graciously declined the offer. The police eventually became involved, and the sturgeon ended its days in the Natural History Museum.

Just in case you are thinking of catching a whale or sturgeon to make an offering to the Royal household, you better be advised that they are also now covered under an international treaty and classed as protected species, making it illegal to catch or kill them deliberately.

The King is Permitted to Drive Without a Driver's Licence

All motorists and motorcyclists using a vehicle on public highways require a driver's licence. This is standard practice and a legal requirement. Driving a vehicle without a licence is an offence. The law applies to all drivers and motorcyclists, with one exception. His Majesty The King is not required to have a driver's license, even if he chooses to drive on a public road. This is because all driver's licences are issued in The King's name.

This was the same also for the previous monarch, Queen Elizabeth II. In fact, whereas King Charles took his driving test whilst he was Prince of Wales, Her late Majesty was never required to take a test or carry a driver's licence.

Following his accession to the throne, The King no longer requires a driver's licence. However, his wife, The Queen Consort Camilla, still requires a licence.

The King Does Not Need a Passport

Since passports first came into existence during the reign of King Henry V in 1414, they have been issued in the name of the monarch. As each passport is issued in his name, it would be unnecessary for The King to carry his own as he would be able just to say, "*I grant myself safe conduct.*" Until the death of Her late Majesty Queen Elizabeth II, all passports carried a diplomatic request requiring the bearer be afforded free passage without let or hindrance, as requested by "*Her

Majesty." All new passports will now be issued in the name of *"His Majesty"* King Charles III.

All other Royal family members are still required to carry a passport when travelling. This was also the case when The King himself was Prince of Wales.

The Four 'O'Clock Punishment Parade

Most people, I'm sure, will agree that watching the Changing of the Guard at Buckingham Palace is a wondrous sight to behold. There is a lesser-known parade that occurs just around the corner on the courtyard in front of Horse Guards at 4pm each day. This is known as the Dismount Parade. Over the years, it has also acquired the nicknames of '*The Four'O'Clock Parade*' or '*Punishment Parade*'.

During this daily 4pm parade, the mounted Household Cavalry soldiers guarding the official Whitehall entrance to Buckingham Palace are inspected by an officer. The mounted guards then dismount and lead their horses back to the stables whilst they are relieved by two dismounted soldiers. These dismounted soldiers will continue to guard the entrance until 8pm when the main gates to Horse Guards are closed. One soldier will remain on guard duty in the courtyard, being replaced each hour throughout the night until 7am, when the gates are re-opened to the public.

This curious additional parade began in 1894 and quickly earned the nickname 'punishment parade' because of how it came about. One day in 1894, Queen Victoria rode through Horse Guards in London and decided to inspect her troops. She was shocked to discover the entire guard drinking and gambling whilst on duty. So angered by what she had seen, The Queen decided to punish them. She ordered the whole guard to be inspected daily at 4pm by an officer for the next 100 years.

The punishment finally came to an end in 1994. However, Queen Elizabeth II decided that she would like the Dismount Parade to continue, no longer as a form of punishment but as a tradition. It continues to this day.

Illegal to Refuse a Knighthood

Receiving recognition from The Crown is one of the highest honours that a person could achieve. It does then raise the question, why would anyone wish to reject such an honour?

This can happen for various reasons. Some previous recipients have rejected an honour only to accept another higher honour later. In 1986, children's novelist Roald Dahl turned down an OBE, allegedly because he was holding out for a knighthood. Some refuse just because it doesn't fit with their beliefs. Notably, in 2015, the musician John Lydon (Johnny Rotten) stated, *"Oh, they're trying to give me an OBE or an MBE or whatever that is. Nope, not interested."*

People can reject honours with relative ease these days, and it is no longer an offence to refuse a knighthood. Between 1951 and 1999, 277 people refused honours from The Crown. Famous Lancashire painter L.S. Lowry rejected an honour more times than anyone else, turning down five honours, including a knighthood.

It hasn't always been this way. Centuries ago, it was considered so insulting to The Crown that anyone who rejected a knighthood was harshly punished. One such incident occurred in 1233, when Roger de Somerie, Baron of Dudley, was summoned to the Royal court to appear before King Henry III. Roger of Dudley failed to attend to receive this Royal honour of a knighthood, which brought with it significant personal expense in those days. The King was furious and ordered that Roger's mansion, along with any houses and land that he owned, was seized by The Crown.

Other notable people who have more recently declined a knighthood include the musician David Bowie who refused a knighthood in 2003 and previously declined a CBE in 2000. The film and theatre director Danny Boyle refused a knighthood in 2013. Author Rudyard Kipling twice declined a knighthood, both in 1899 and 1903.

On a more joyous occasion, in 1965, the Beatles were awarded MBEs for their services to music and culture. This did cause outrage in some quarters, with people surprised to see pop stars being honoured. John Lennon defended their position at the time by publicly commenting, *"Lots of people who complained about us getting the MBE received theirs for heroism in the war. They got them for killing people. We got ours for entertaining. I'd say we deserve ours more."* Three years later, Lennon famously returned his MBE to Buckingham Palace to protest the government's involvement in a war.

Illegal to Draw Blood Within The Royal Palaces

In what appears to be a very civilised (it is, after all, in the King's household) but nonetheless gruesome process, the Royal court had a particular way of dealing with those who had a fight and drew blood in Royal residences. The offender would be invited to a private silver service dinner party, where their right hand would be cut off.

In 1541, King Henry VIII passed a law which applied to anyone who, whilst in any of the Royal palaces, maliciously hit another person "*against the King's Peace*" and drew blood in the process. It was introduced to deter poor manners and instil discipline among staff in the Royal households.

No expense was spared for the guilty party. It was a full white glove service with the finest food, wine, silverware and linen available in the Royal household. In this horrendous yet civilised form of sentencing, many staff are on hand to play their part. If this wasn't horrific enough, once the offender's right-hand is chopped off, he must also pay a fine to The King and gets to spend the rest of his life staring at the walls in prison.

The law states in excruciating detail, strictly how this bizarre ritual should be carried out, as follows:

"And for the further declaration of the solemn and due circumstance of the execution appertaining and of long time used and accustomed, to and for such malicious strikings, by reason whereof blood is, hath been, or hereafter shall be shed against the King's peace. It is therefore enacted by the authority aforesaid, that the Sergeant or Chief Surgeon for the time being, or his deputy of the King's household, his heirs and successors, shall be ready at the time and place of execution, as shall be appointed as is aforesaid, to sear the stump when the hand is stricken off.

And the Sergeant of the Pantry ... shall be also then and there ready to give bread to the party that shall have his hand so stricken off.

And the Sergeant of the Cellar ... shall also be then and there ready with a pot of red wine to give the same party drink after his hand is so stricken off and the stump seared.

And the Sergeant of the Ewry ... shall also be then and there ready with cloths sufficient for the Surgeon to occupy about the same execution.

And the Yeoman of the Chandry ... shall also be then and there, and have in readiness seared cloths sufficient for the Surgeon to occupy about the same execution.

And the Master Cook ... shall be also then and there ready, and bring with him a dressing knife, and shall deliver the same knife at the place of execution to the Sergeant of the Larder ... who shall be also then and there ready, and hold upright the dressing knife till execution be done.

And the Sergeant of the Poultry ... shall be also then and there ready with a cock in his hand, ready for the Surgeon to wrap about the same stump, when the hand shall be so stricken off.

And the Yeoman of the Scullery ... to be also then and there ready, and prepare and make at the place of execution a fire of coals, and there to make ready searing-irons against the said Surgeon or his deputy shall occupy the same.

And the Sergeant or Chief Farrier ... shall be also then and there ready, and bring with him the searing-irons, and deliver the same to the same Sergeant or Chief Surgeon or to his deputy when they be hot.

And the Groom of the Salcery ... shall be also then and there ready with vinegar and cold water, and give attendance upon the said Surgeon or his deputy until the same execution be done.

And the Sergeant of the Woodyard ... shall bring to the said place of execution a block, with a betil, a staple, and cords to bind the said hand upon the block while the execution is in doing."

Bizarrely, this brutal law was only repealed in 1967. That was the same year that The Beatles released their famous Sgt. Pepper's Lonely Hearts Club Band album!

Keeper of The King's Swans

Swans have retained their status as Royal birds under the Royal prerogative since the 12th century. This was the first legal mention of the Royal prerogative over mute swans. Following this, in 1482-1483, King Edward IV passed a law to address the increase in the number of stolen swans and cygnets, where people unlawfully marked them as their property. This law referred to the proper marking of swans to ensure they were identified as the property of the rightful owners. The Swan marks were small nicks cut into the swan's upper beak. The marks of various families were then documented in Swan Rolls.

The whole matter was taken very seriously as swan thefts began to rise during the mediaeval period. Special courts were set up to deal with questions over a swan's ownership. These were known as 'Swan Motes'.

A new law passed in 1971 preserved the monarch's rights of ownership over mute swans. Today, The King holds the title *'Seigneur of the Swans'*.

This is something that the Royal household, even to this day, takes seriously, and there is an official Royal post held by a designated person who looks after The King's swans. This post has existed since the 13th century, when the first known Keeper of The King's Swans was appointed. In 1993, this post was split into two new roles: the *Warden of the Swans* and the *Marker of the Swans*.

Illegal to Affix a Stamp On An Envelope Upside Down

There is a common belief that placing a postage stamp upside down on an envelope or package is illegal. The belief is derived from the fact that postage stamps in the UK depict an image of the current monarch. It is thought that if you were to place a stamp upside down, that would be the equivalent of putting The King's image upside down. The mind boggles when you consider that only a few years ago, one would have to lick the rear of the postage stamp before affixing it to a package.

This belief is founded on the premise that doing anything that would incorrectly display His Majesty's image would be considered treason under a law from 1848. The punishment for this offence was to be "*transported beyond the seas for the term of his or her natural life.*" Since penal transportation stopped in 1868, the sentence is now just to spend the rest of your life in prison.

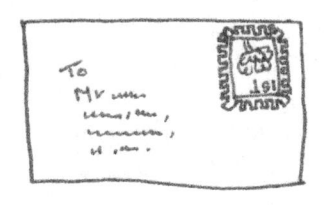

This would be utterly bizarre if it were true, but it just isn't. The law itself is genuine and features elsewhere in this book. However, it does not refer to postage stamps. The Royal Mail and The Law Commission have also confirmed that placing a postage stamp upside down would not be considered an offence of treason.

Treason!

'Treason' is a term that is often thrown around, although not as much as during earlier centuries. We've all most likely heard of famous people throughout history that have been tried and executed for Treason. People like Guy Fawkes, Catherine Howard (Henry VIII's fifth wife) and Sir. Walter Raleigh.

Treason is an offence. It always has been and, most likely, always will be. In law, there are two types of treason: *High Treason* and *Petty Treason*.

High treason is considered the most serious offence and is essentially a crime of disloyalty towards the Crown. This included things like plotting the Sovereign's murder; raising a war against the Sovereign; and giving aid and comfort to the Sovereign's enemies. Over the centuries, various other crimes have been categorised as high treason, including making fake money and even being a Catholic priest. Petty treason is where a crime is committed against one of the Sovereign's subjects. This would be, for example, the murder of a legal superior. It dealt with offences of the murder of a master by a servant, the murder of a husband by his wife, or the murder of a Bishop by one of his clergy. Petty Treason ceased to exist from 1828 onwards. Since then, any discussion of 'treason' has referred to High Treason.

In 1348, Sir. John Gerberge of Royston was charged with the crime of treason after falsely imprisoning William de Boletisford and taking his horse until he paid him £90. The powerful land barons encouraged King Edward III to pass a law to specifically define what treason was. As a result, in 1351, The Treason Act was passed.

The punishment for treason was death. More often than not, the method of death was through torture. The required execution method for men in England was to be hanged, drawn and quartered.

The traitor's body parts would then be publicly displayed on a gibbet as a cautionary reminder to the local townsfolk about what happens to traitors. This remained the required sentence until 1814 when instead, the traitor would be hanged until dead.

Such a punishment was considered too brutal for women. Instead, they were drawn and then burned alive at the stake. Catherine Murphy was the last woman to be burned for high treason in 1789. A year later, the sentence was replaced by the Treason Act (1790), after which women were hanged until dead.

Capital punishment (death) still remained the penalty for high treason until 1998.

The Home Secretary Had to Be Present at All Royal Births

Since 1894, the Home Secretary would have to be present at the birth of any Royal babies. This was to verify that proceedings were handled correctly and ensure the baby wasn't swapped at birth. As intrusive as this may seem, before this, it wouldn't just be the Home Secretary, but a whole host of Privy councillors and ministers would have to witness the birth. This would be in addition to the ladies-in-waiting and any medical staff in attendance.

This has no foundations in law but is derived from a custom originating from the reign of King James II. When his wife, Queen Mary of Modena, gave birth to their son James Francis Edward Stuart, on 10th June 1688, rumours abounded that this was not their son. Many believed this baby, an imposter, had been secretly brought into the room through a hidden wall panel at St. James's Palace or smuggled into the chamber in a warming pan.

It is likely this rumour came about as a result of anti-Catholic feelings at the time. King James II had converted to Catholicism a decade before, and people feared another Catholic dynasty. The rumour was spread that The Queen's child had died at birth and another baby had been smuggled into the room to become the heir to the throne. Despite this, seventy prominent figures were present during the birth, which all attested there was no funny business.

As a result of this episode, it was decided that all Royal births would, from that point onwards, be witnessed by several eminent politicians to verify the child's claim as rightful heir to the throne. This practice continued long into the 20th century.

In 1894, when the future Queen Mary gave birth to Prince Edward (later to become King Edward VIII), Queen Victoria decided that this was an unnecessary fuss and that only the Home Secretary should be required in attendance.

This custom occurred for the final time during the birth of Princess Alexandra on Christmas Day in 1936, witnessed by Home Secretary Sir. John Simon.

When Princess Elizabeth (later The Queen) gave birth to our current King Charles III, her father, King George VI, decided to put a stop to this custom. From that moment on, a Home Secretary was no longer required to be present at Royal births.

Chapter Twenty

TRADES

Working and trade are the bedrock of our great nation of explorers, pioneers and industrialists.

Remarkably, barbers and surgeons are cut from the same cloth. Barbers used to carry out rudimentary surgery and were also dentists. Thankfully, you no longer need to go through the gruesome ordeal of being covered in leeches for a bit of bloodletting each time you visit the barber and feeling a little under the weather. Although, a visit to the GP may see you returning with shopping bags full of peppers, radishes and spices. Amusingly, a law had to be passed to prevent barbers from practising surgery and surgeons from cutting hair.

And remember, the next time you answer the door to the postal worker, don't engage them in idle gossip. You may be risking a trip to the magistrate's court.

Talking to The 'Postman' Could Land You In Prison

The laws surrounding the Post Office date back to the sixteenth century when in 1516, King Henry VII established the role of Master of the Posts. This role continued until it was finally abolished in 1969. It wasn't until 1635 that King Charles I made the postal service available to all, not just the wealthy. Oddly though, from the beginning, the recipient paid the postage costs, not the sender. With the amount of junk mail we all receive these days, most of us would be penniless in months if this were still the case!

It is now an offence to open post belonging to another person if you know or suspect it has been incorrectly delivered to you. This includes mail sent to your address meant for a previous householder. Royal Mail advises under such circumstances that the envelope should be marked 'Return to Sender' and placed in any post box.

It is also an offence to intentionally delay the post without reasonable excuse. So be warned the next time you engage your postal worker in inane chit-chat about the weather. Amusingly, it is also an offence to display any writing signs or images of a post box, in or on your house, in such a way that members of the public may believe it to be a public post box.

So, what happens in the cases where the mail has been delivered through your door, and you innocently open it in a hurry, not reading the address label? Well, you'll be pleased to know that you haven't committed an offence because the law requires some criminal intent in doing so. In this case, it was done innocently and unknowingly, so you can rest easy at night.

Half a Dozen Red Peppers, Some Rosemary & Remove My Gall Bladder Please

Apothecaries used to be ordinary grocers. The term 'apothecary' is derived from the Latin word *apotheca*, meaning a place where wine, spices and herbs were stored. This became the commonplace term to describe those who kept a stock of wines and spices for sale to the public. Apothecaries in London can be traced back to the Guild of Pepperers, which was formed in the City of London in 1180. By 1316, the Guild of Pepperers had joined with the Spicers, and in 1428 both became incorporated as the Worshipful Company of Grocers, selling wholesale to grocery merchants.

Rolling the clock forward, the spicer-apothecaries had become the equivalent of our modern-day high street chemist shops, preparing and selling medicines by the mid-sixteenth century. This caused a conflict with the College of Physicians, who felt they had authority over medical matters. For several years, the London apothecaries, with their specialist pharmacy skills, sought to leave the Worshipful Company of Grocers and establish their own guild or livery. Fortunately for them, their leader, Gideon de Laune was personal apothecary to Anne of Denmark, the wife of King James I. Shortly afterwards, on 6th December 1617, The Worshipful Society of Apothecaries was incorporated by Royal charter.

In 1815, King George III passed a law known as the Apothecaries Act. This finally recognised apothecaries as medical practitioners and enabled the Society to license doctors to practise Medicine. This led to the evolution of the old apothecaries into what we now see as general practitioners (GPs).

Barbers May Not Practice Surgery & Surgeons May Not Cut Hair

In 1540 King Henry VIII passed the Barbers and Surgeons Act when the Fellowship of Surgeons merged with the Barbers' Company, forming the Company of Barbers and Surgeons. This Act made it illegal for Barbers to practise surgery and for surgeons to cut hair. Peculiarly, however, both barbers and surgeons were still permitted to work as dentists, extracting teeth. As a further point of interest, barbers received higher pay than surgeons around this time.

In those early years, bleeding or blood letting was the answer to most ailments, and monks would regularly practice as barber-surgeons, looking after both the physical and spiritual aspects of their parishioners. This became very profitable for the church. However, this changed when Pope Innocent II banned clergymen from practising medicine. In 1163, Pope Alexander III also declared that clergymen getting their hands bloody was contrary to the practice of spiritual healing. He banned religious orders from shedding blood. Blood letting at the time was seen as very important. Patients would often be bled to the point of fainting. Blood letting was used as a standard cure for depression and love-sickness.

Barbers would advertise their services by placing a bowl of blood in their shop windows. They also advertised their dental treatments by adorning their shop walls with strings of pulled teeth. In 1307, the City of London banned barbers from placing bowls of blood in their shop windows. The creepy teeth were just fine! They required all collected blood to be taken to the River Thames and dumped into the water. To get around this, barbers instead advertised by placing red rags in their windows. This was the early version of what we now see as the barber's shop pole.

Another peculiar aspect of the history of barbers relates to the origin of the barber's pole. This can be traced back to the Middle Ages when barbers regularly engaged in blood letting. The red on the barber's pole represents the blood, and the white represents the bandages used to stop the blood flow. The pole symbolises a stick that patients sometimes squeeze to make their veins stand out more prominently. In America, barber's poles are often red, white and blue. The addition of the blue colour is most likely symbolic of the veins that were cut during the blood letting procedure.

Records show that in 1308, the City of London had a Barbers' Guild.

In 1540, a law was passed changing the Guild's title to Barber-Surgeon. King Henry VIII stated that barbers in the City of London should not operate any surgery in their shop, including the letting of blood. They were still permitted to draw teeth on the same premises. Despite this, barbers continued to perform surgical procedures, eventually using leeches for blood letting, which was considered a more civilised approach. Not to be outdone, surgeons also continued to practice barbery.

In 1745, a new law was passed which created the two separate organisations, the Barbers of London and the Surgeons of London. The Surgeons guild later became what is now the Royal College of Surgeons.

Turning a Blind Eye to Piracy

A law was passed by King George I due to increased piracy acts and robberies at sea against his ships. It required all masters, commanders, officers or seamen to defend themselves against pirates or forfeit their wages and suffer six months of imprisonment. This law was only repealed as recently as 1993.

Chapter Twenty-One
Witchcraft & Other Sorcery

In today's world, if you see a witch walking towards you on the street, it's either a schoolchild dressed for World Book Day or Halloween. Either way, there's no reason to be alarmed.

That wasn't always the case, as we'll see. Centuries ago, there used to be mass paranoia, and the slightest little thing that went wrong would be blamed on witchcraft and sorcery.

There were often perfectly innocent and scientific explanations behind what was once considered witchcraft.

In this chapter, we delve back in time through the world of witches, sorcery and ghosts.

You would be astonished to learn just how recent the last cases of witchcraft in the UK were.

Illegal to Pretend to be a Ghost

While no specific law makes it illegal for you to pretend to be a ghost, whether in public or private, we know from recent reports that doing so is not such a good idea.

We earlier examined the story of the Hammersmith Ghost, an innocent man who was shot for being a ghost. More recently, in 2014, a man from Portsmouth was arrested after loitering in Kingston Cemetery and pretending to be a ghost, waving his arms around, making spooky noises and shouting, "*Wooooo*." Nearby mourners overheard and were distressed by his outlandish behaviour. The police were called, and he was promptly arrested for *"using threatening or abusive words or behaviour likely to cause distress."* For his ghoulish behaviour, he was fined.

Illegal to Resurrect a Corpse

When King James I arrived in England, the country was already in a state of paranoia about witchcraft and sorcery. It was like living in the land of Hogwarts! He believed the English Crown had been easy on those accused of witchcraft. To tighten the laws surrounding it, he decided to stamp his mark and passed a new witchcraft law in 1604.

This new law fed into the public paranoia and increased the severity of punishment given to all those found guilty. It was now an offence to resurrect any *'dead man, woman, or child out of his, her, or their grave, or any other place where the dead body resteth ... to be employed or used in any manner of witchcraft, sorcery, charm, or enchantment ... shall suffer the pains of death as a felon or felons, and shall lose the privilege and benefit of clergy and sanctuary.'*

Looking at this law in the modern world context, it seems simply outrageous. Still, you have to remember these were the times of the mass witch trials and the upcoming Lancaster Witch Trials (1612–1634).

In fact, the self-styled Witch-Finder General Matthew Hopkins used this law to pass judgement on 'witches' during his brief reign of terror in East Anglia between 1644 and his death in 1647.

Illegal to be a Witch

Witches, conjuring and sorcery have been part of our history for centuries. It was initially seen as a crime against humanity.

That later changed during the Puritan period in the 16th and 17th centuries, when it was seen more as a crime against God.

To understand the effects of witchcraft on the public, from the paranoia of the witch trials to the modern-day Hogwarts school societies run by children, we must take a brief but colourful walk through history.

It wasn't until the reign of King Æthelstan (924-939) that we saw the first death penalty for murder committed by acts of witchcraft by way of 'witch swimming'. This was the practice of tying up the accused witch and dunking them into a river to see whether they would sink or float. If they sank, this was an indication of their innocence. If they floated, it indicated the accused was indeed a witch.

The first woman accused of sorcery in England was Agnes, the wife of Odo, who in 1209 opted for trial by ordeal. She was freed after grasping a red-hot iron and surviving, proving her innocence.

Initially, the religious courts would try the accused and then hand them over to authorities to face punishment. The punishment was far less severe when the civil courts started handling witchcraft cases in the 14th century. For example, in 1371, a man was arrested for possessing a skull, the head of a corpse and a grimoire (a book containing incantations and magical rites). He was released after promising never again to perform magical spells, and his props were publicly burned.

In 1542, amidst religious tensions, King Henry VIII passed the first Witchcraft Act, specifically making witchcraft a felony and carrying the penalty of death.

In 1563, Queen Elizabeth I passed her Witchcraft Act (*An Act Against Conjurations, Enchantments And Witchcrafties*). The

Act stated, "... *if any person or persons ... shall use, practise or exercise any Witchcraft, Enchantment, Charm or Sorcery, whereby any person shall happen to be killed or destroyed*", they shall be guilty of a felony and suffer the pain of death.

King James I passed his Witchcraft law in 1604. This brought the death penalty for anyone who used or practised invocations or conjurations with any evil and wicked spirit.

In June 1727, Janet Horne was the last person to be executed in Britain for witchcraft. She was burned at the stake in Dornoch, Scotland. Her neighbours had been gossiping and believed Janet was a witch because her daughter suffered a deformity of the hands and feet, making her look like she had horses hooves. Janet was accused of turning her daughter into a pony to enable her to ride around the countryside carrying out her incantations.

In the intervening years, there wasn't very much by way of witchcraft until May 1944. This was the very high-profile case of Helen Duncan. She was the last person to be found guilty under the Witchcraft law of 1735, and sent to prison for witchcraft. 'Hellish Nell', as she was known, was sentenced to spend nine months at His Majesty's Pleasure.

Her crime was not one of witchcraft but more concerning the pretence of witchcraft. She had been charging people money to attend her séances and was caught defrauding them on more than one occasion.

Her downfall came during a séance in which she claimed that a sailor had appeared and announced that his ship HMS Barham had just been sunk. Unfortunately for Hellish Nell, HMS Barham had been sunk by a German U-boat on 25th November 1941 with the loss of all crew aboard. The sinking of HMS Barham was classified as a secret at the time by The Admiralty.

Her trial was conducted at The Old Bailey, where she was sentenced for Witchcraft, to nine months imprisonment at Holloway prison. She tried to appeal the sentence, but The House of Lords denied the appeal. Prime Minister Winston Churchill wrote a memo to Home Secretary Herbert Morrison, referring to the matter as 'obsolete tomfoolery'.

Whilst Helen Duncan was the last person to be convicted and imprisoned, she wasn't the last person in the UK to be sentenced as a 'witch.' That was Jane Rebecca Yorke, a 72-year-old woman from Forest Gate, London.

Illegal to Feed a Witch's Cat

In 1603, King James I came down from Scotland and took the throne upon the death of Queen Elizabeth I. A year later, he passed a new Witchcraft law.

This now made it an offence to not only engage in practices of witchcraft but also merely to seek the help of witches or fortune tellers. It included the crime of helping anyone engaged in fortune-telling, witchcraft or sorcery.

The penalty for this offence was the same, whether you were entertaining evil and wicked spirits, merely attending a fortune telling or helping someone else to attend. Interestingly, this law made it an offence to feed what can be considered a 'witch's familiar'. So, if you happen to be doing a community-minded service and feeding your neighbour's cat whilst they were away, and the local community felt the cat's owner was part of a witch's coven, then you've committed this offence of feeding their cat. The penalty for these offences, including attending a fortune telling or feeding a witch's familiar, was death.

Illegal to Pretend to be a Witch ... But No Longer Illegal to Actually be a Witch

In the reign of King George II, a new Witchcraft law was passed by Parliament in 1735, which marked a change in the attitudes towards witchcraft and repealed most of the previous witchcraft laws.

The intention was to show the public that witches were a thing of the past and no longer existed. Essentially, it was no longer illegal to be a witch.

It made it an offence for any person to "... *pretend to exercise or use any kind of Witchcraft, Sorcery, Inchantment, or Conjuration, or undertake to tell Fortunes, or pretend, from his or her Skill or Knowledge in any occult or crafty Science...*"

The penalty for those found guilty of pretending to be a witch was to be imprisoned for one year, and every three months, they would have to stand in the local pillory for one hour.

This 1735 Witchcraft law remained in force until 1951.

ACKNOWLEDGMENTS

I would like to thank all those who so generously gave up their time to help with the production of this book and helping in translating my thoughts from paper to print.

I would also like to record my thanks and appreciation for the help and support received from the following:

(In alphabetical order)

Ms. Caitlin Williams (for Welsh translations)

Councillor Neil Darby - Mayor of Preston

The Curators of His Majesty's Historic Royal Palaces

HM Treasury, Debt and Reserves Management department

Lancaster City Council

Napthens Solicitors (Blackburn)

Mr. Nicholas Wood - Honorary Curator of
The Worshipful Society of Apothecaries of London

The Staff at The British Library, London

The Bank of England

BIZARRE LAWS OF THE UK FOR KIDS

The Librarians at The Law Society, London

His Majesty's The Royal Mint

The Rt. Hon Sir Robert Buckland KBE KC MP

Tuckers Solicitors (Manchester)

Mr. William Hunt, TD BA FCA -
former Windsor Herald, College of Arms

The Yeoman Warders of His Majesty's Royal Palace
and Fortress of the Tower of London

I would like to give a special mention to The Rt. Hon. Nigel Evans MP, Deputy Speaker (House of Commons), who helped immensely in supporting this project, as a great advocate of children's rights.

Most of all, thanks to my father, Fabian Lord, without whom this book would simply not have been written. I am deeply appreciative of his constant interest, encouragement and support in completing this book.

PERMISSIONS

Excerpts from judgements and statutes are Crown copyright defined under Section 163 of the Copyright, Designs and Patents Act (1988). Any Crown copyright material is reproduced with the permission of the Controller of The Office of Public Sector Information (OPSI) and the King's Printer for Scotland. Some quotations may be licensed under the terms of the Open Government Licence (http://www.nationalarchives.gov.uk/doc/open-government-licence/version/3).

All images used are either owned by the author or in the public domain.

NOTE ON THE TYPESET

The text of this book is set in Libre Caslon, a digital typeface of the Serif classification, designed by Pablo Impallari in 2012. Libre Caslon is a revival of the 18th-century William Caslon classic design, based on the alluring hand-lettered American Caslons typical of 1950s advertising.

ABOUT AUTHOR

Montgomery (Monty) Lord is a multi award-winning change maker, social entrepreneur and researcher dedicated to challenging injustices through the use of law. Described as an exemplar for making positive changes that impact on the community, he was named in The Independent newspaper (The Happy List 20/21) as in the top 50 inspirational people driving positive change in Britain.

Over recent years, Monty has engaged thousands of children across several countries in his ground-breaking research and was recognised with the Prime Minister's Points of Lights Award, the Diana Award, the Platinum Champion Award and the British Citizen Youth Award for services to the community & charity.

At the age of 7 years old, Monty had already released his first book and became, at the time, the UK's youngest bestselling author. He is a member of the Royal Society of Literature.

Monty maintains a keen interest in both law and history. At the age of 14, taking a semester-long distance learning course from Yale University. He developed his memory techniques (Rapid Memory Recall System®) which he later used to gain 5 Guinness World Records as a world memory champion.

In 2020, at the age of 14, he founded the national registered charity Young Active Minds. The aim is to promote education inequality & mental health awareness throughout all schools & community groups, irrespective of current attainment levels or cultural diversity of the students.

In 2021, as a world memory champion, Monty went on to become the youngest person in the UK with the most world records. He still holds that title.

Despite the constant label in the media, Monty strenuously rejects the title 'genius', claiming anyone can be a genius with some resilience and a little perseverance. He strongly believes that a good memory is not predicated on a person's intellect and that anyone can have a good memory.

An accomplished public speaker, Monty has spoken at TEDx talks events and at the age of 14, presented his 55,000-word research thesis to world leaders at the United Nations in Geneva and the All-Party Parliamentary Group on Mentoring. Monty has been involved with several published university research articles.

He has been devoting much of his free time independently over the last few years to not only helping those with mental health disorders but also raising awareness of mental health issues, saving people from suicide and depression, bringing about positive change and making life better for many others in the community. In his spare time, he creates and releases music under his music label, primarily Lo-Fi beats in support of mental health awareness.

Monty has led several campaigns, raising awareness of the United Nations Sustainable Development Goals. He formed the United Nations Association in Bolton and now chairs the group.

At the age of 16, he established Young Legal Eagles® to promote the rights, views and interests of children and young people and the Rule of Law in policies or decisions affecting their lives. Young Legal Eagles® provides legal information to children and young people, through printed and electronic media. Monty conducts the legal research, develops and publishes the guidance booklets and videos in multiple languages to benefit a wider public footprint. He took this national initiative to No.10 Downing Street with a view to integrating children's rights into the national curriculum. In December 2022, Monty spoke about children's rights as a panel speaker at Amnesty International. He later presented his findings at the United Nations in Geneva.

He created the short-documentary 'Do Children Have Rights?' With the help of a dedicated team of translators, the documentary was translated into multiple languages to help raise awareness of children's rights across all communities. The documentary was aired on Amazon Fire TV.

In his first legal case, at the age of 16, he represented 6 claimants bringing an action for breach of contract against a large national youth organisation, for multiple instances of bullying and abuse against their own staff and young cadets. He took the matter to the County Court with 85 exhibits and 317 pages of statements. The organisation decided to settle out of court, paying full damages and court fees.

As a supporter of several charities, Monty is an ambassador for both the #iWill Campaign and the British Citizen Awards and a trustee and schools engagement officer for Young Active Minds. He sat on the Diana Award judging panel and is a member of the National Anti-Bullying Youth Board. Monty sits on the committee of Amnesty UK's Children's Human Rights Network.

In recognition of his 'outstanding contribution' to volunteering, Monty was awarded the Platinum Champion Award by Her Majesty The Queen Consort and invited to the Platinum Party at Buckingham Palace.

In his free time, Monty enjoys running, swimming and Taek-won-Do, achieving black belt from an early age.

The national media has followed and widely reported upon many of Monty's various projects over the last few years, with widespread coverage on BBC & ITV News, radio and both broadsheet & tabloid newspapers.

Printed in Great Britain
by Amazon